Lost Villages
Found Communities

A Pictorial History
of the Lost Villages
of the
St. Lawrence Seaway

by Anne-Marie L. Shields
2004

Canadian Cataloguing in Publication Data
National Library of Canada Cataloguing in Publication

Léveillé-Shields, Anne-Marie
    Lost Villages, Found Communities: A Pictorial History of the Lost Villages of the St. Lawrence Seaway / by Anne-Marie L. Shields

Includes bibliographical references.
ISBN 0-9733630-0-2

    1. Ontario, Eastern–History, Local. 2. Saint Lawrence Seaway–History.
    3. Historic buildings–Ontario, Eastern. 4. Historic buildings–Ontario, Eastern–Pictorial works.
    5. Architecture, Domestic–Ontario, Eastern–History. 1. Title.

FC3095.E25L48 2004   971.3'7   C2004-902457-4

Cover design, book layout, and artwork: Anne-Marie L. Shields
Printed in Cornwall, Ontario, Canada

Printed by Astro Printing Service (Cornwall) Ltd.

With Love
to
Susie, Pierre, Dominique
Jennifer, Samantha
Sara, Sophie
Jeremy
Yvan, Martine, Richard

Acknowledgements

It is with sincere appreciation to the communities who warmly welcomed me three years ago that I was able to write and illustrate this heritage book.

I am most grateful to the members of the Lost Villages Historical Society, especially to Jim Brownell, past president (1992 -2003) of the Historical Society and Curator of the Lost Villages Museum, for their support and their great enthusiasm for the project. The assistance of Jane Craig, President of the Society, as well as that of Alan Rafuse, archivist for the Society, has been most appreciated.

The contribution of Peter D. Cazaly, Research Officer for the Upper Canada Village Museum, has been a great asset for my book and has been truly appreciated. I thank Shaun Wallace, President of Morrisburg Historical Society, and Joyce Fader, President of Iroquois Historical Society, for their editing for accuracy and their willingness to share their knowledge and expertise. I also thank the members of the Societies for their comments and suggestions.

Along the way, I received precious assistance from many people who were former residents of the Lost Villages and who witnessed the upheaval of 1954 - 1958. I am most grateful to the people who welcomed me into their communities and who were so willing to share their personal stories. Their comments have been a source of inspiration for my artistic endeavours.

I wish to thank my best friend, Robert McEwen, for his assistance and his many precious comments along the way. Although every effort has been made to be accurate, I apologize for any errors and omissions, as they are mine only. I hope you will enjoy reading **'The Lost Villages, Found Communities: A Pictorial History of the Lost Villages of the St. Lawrence Seaway'** as much as I enjoyed creating it.

I wish to acknowledge and express my sincere appreciation to the following generous donors for their precious financial support. They are James Brownell, MPP, Patti Chevers, Domtar Inc., Barbara and Ray Fenton, The McIntosh Country Inn & Conference Centre (Tom Morrow - Owner/General Manager), Nahsila Freight Services, and Traer Van Allen, M.D.

Anne-Marie L. Shields

Preface

The book is titled *'Lost Villages, Found Communities: A Pictorial History of the Lost Villages of the St. Lawrence Seaway'* to honour the people who lost their villages in 1954 and who found within themselves the courage and inner strength to build new communities and, indeed, establish new roots. In the face of change, like their ancestors more than two hundred years ago, they found fortitude and resilience. They followed in the footsteps of their pioneer ancestors and became the new pioneers of the St. Lawrence Seaway and Power Project.

This pictorial history is a celebration of the community spirit which was especially challenged, before, during, and after the construction of the Seaway in 1958. It is written as a means to document history as well as to be a testimony of the rich heritage of the Eastern Ontario riverside communities. In addition, it hopes to rekindle fond memories of former neighbours and friends. Moreover, it hopes to be a visual history of the contributions of the people who played a significant part of the Canadian Heritage.

It is hoped that through my drawings and watercolour illustrations of the lost, moved, or newly built homes, and through my research of the archival documentation, a new appreciation of the inner soul and strength of character of our ancestors will surface. In addition, it is my objective to make more tangible the creative energy and undaunting spirit of a whole people who lived on the shores of the St. Lawrence River. Taken as a whole, the story of the people connected to the homes offers a snapshot of the historic riverside communities and the impact of the Seaway and Power Project on their lives.

The selection of homes was most challenging for a number of reasons. A meeting with members of the Lost Villages Museum Historical Society, the Morrisburg and Iroquois Historical Societies, a selected review of the societies' archives, as well as of those of Upper Canada Village Museum, and a perusal of the local libraries historical documentation have greatly influenced my choice. There are many more homes which, either by their history, by their architecture, or by their uniqueness, could have been included. However, space has been the limiting factor. In spite of the poor quality of some of the photographs and records as a source of information for artistic purpose, some unique homes were included.

A decision to include less than seventy homes was further limiting. Although the generosity of the past, as well as the present, owners of these homes, who volunteered personal stories was greatly appreciated, a selection of the most interesting and unique stories was made. Moreover, a sufficient number of homes to include in such a pictorial history was important to tell an interesting and factual story. The selected homes are those which typify a part of the story of the riverside communities and their people. It is, by no means, the whole story, but rather a cross-section of the geographic, historic, and architectural heritage left by our ancestors and built upon by their descendants. It is a small part of the local history which forms a significant part of our Canadian history.

The book is divided into three parts. Part One titled **"We Were Here"** introduces the reader to the geography and history of the riverside communities prior to 1954, and to the Seaway and Power Projects, and the impact of the project upon the lives of the people and their homes. Part Two titled **"Lost Villages"** tells the story of each lost village and specific homes which characterize the pioneering spirit. Part Three titled **"Found Communities"** reviews a number of aspects of the newly created communities and the heritage left after the Seaway and Power project.

Foreword

Lost Villages: Found Communities

On July 1, 1958, dynamite tore open the last cofferdam and the water of the St. Lawrence River rolled over the farmlands and communities that hugged the river in the old Royal Townships of Cornwall, Osnabruck, Williamsburg, and Matilda. For fifty years now, the thoughts and memories of gentler times and days along the St. Lawrence River return to the minds of those who were uprooted from the communities of Aultsville, Farran's Point, Dickinson's Landing, Wales, Moulinette, and Mille Roches; and the hamlets of Woodlands, Santa Cruz, and Maple Grove. A half-century has not faded these memories, and Anne-Marie Shields has captured the history and heritage of those gentler times in Eastern Ontario in her book *LOST VILLAGES: FOUND COMMUNITIES, A Pictorial History of the Lost Villages of the St. Lawrence Seaway.*

Anne-Marie Shields is a relative newcomer to the story of the "Lost Villages", arriving in the Seaway Valley just a few short years ago. It did not take her long, though, to immerse herself in the stories told of the riverfront communities that were displaced by the Hydro and Seaway Projects of the 1950s. Anne-Marie's interest was piqued when stories were told of the pioneer Loyalists who settled the riverfront communities in the late 1700s; of the railroad built to link these towns along the St. Lawrence in the mid-1800s; of the "characters" who gave life to these communities.

Anne-Marie's imagination went into overdrive, and she visioned her book *LOST VILLAGES: FOUND COMMUNITIES,* so capably written and illustrated. Her beautiful watercolours tell the stories of early Eastern Ontario architecture and the people who gave life to these dwellings. Her careful research has added the historical details which span the breadth of Canadian history. During my teaching career, I often mentioned to my students that the history of Eastern Ontario and the "Lost Villages" is imbedded in Canada's historical timeline. Anne-Marie Shields has captured the history and heritage of people and events, her detailed watercolours giving an added dimension to the historical details of her stories. Besides the historical sketches and anecdotes presented by so many of her "new" friends in the Seaway Valley, Anne-Marie has used her literary and artistic talents to capture the essence of these historical, dynamic and, now, lost communities.

Anne-Marie Shields has left no stones unturned in her determination to publish *LOST VILLAGES: FOUND COMMUNITIES.* The Hydro and Seaway engineers left their marks on the landscape of the "Lost Villages", a half-century ago, and Anne-Marie Shields has left her mark on our community, a half-century later. With pen and brush, Anne-Marie Shields has captured the mystique of the "lost" communities of the St. Lawrence communities, and she has given us, through her words, OUR story.

I encourage Anne-Marie and others to keep writing; keep recording; and never let this significant story in Canadian history fade.

Jim Brownell, M.P.P. Stormont, Dundas and Charlottenburgh

Table of Contents

Part one
« We Were Here »

Part Two
« Lost Villages »

Part Three
« Found Communities »

Part One

« We Were Here »

We Were Here

We were here when, in 1954, it was finalized that the St. Lawrence Seaway and Power Project (sometimes referred to as Projects) would become a reality. We were here when plans were made to displace our community and flood our ancestral land. We were living in our riverside communities when the Canadian and the American Governments signed the Agreement which would reshape the international waterways of the St. Lawrence River between Cornwall and Iroquois.

The governments' global plan was to improve the shipping and the navigation channel and harness the potential hydro electric power of the river to meet increasing market demands. The project involved four large agencies across two major countries: The Canadian Seaway Authority, Ontario Hydro, The Power Authority of the State of New York, and The United States Seaway Development Corporation.

The project would result in the flooding of 22,000 acres of land from Cornwall to Iroquois, the displacement of 6,500 people, 530 homes, and, indeed, entire villages as well as the re-shaping of the new shores. Indeed, the project involved three phases: the destruction, the construction, and the rehabilitation of the communities.

The impact of the construction of the St. Lawrence Seaway and Power Project, completed in 1958, on the shore communities from Iroquois to Cornwall was felt by everyone. It was felt in various ways and in various degrees not only because of the magnitude of the project but because of its profound transformation on the lives of the people.

Our homes by the water would be lifted from their foundations, such as we were from our roots, transported to other communities and located on new land to begin their life in a new community. As for those homes which were left behind for various reasons, they are the symbol of a part of ourselves which was uprooted when we started over in our new environment.

One had to say goodbye to the familiar experiences in the old villages: the old village surroundings; the daily events in one's life; the great roar and magnificence of the rapids; the Saturday evenings at the dance pavilion; the Sunday afternoon picnics; the swimming in the river; the family's apple orchard; the busy street where one met friends; the vegetable garden tended with love; the homestead with its unique architecture; the generous neighbour; the small school house; the church where births, marriages, and deaths were celebrated; the view of the canals and all their activities; the old elm tree to which a childhood swing was hanging; the lakeshore view from one's front or back porch; the ancestral land; and, moreover, the sense of belonging to one's own small community.

The only life one had from now on lay ahead. The life one had experienced in one's village would, as of today, be relegated to the domain of memories.

Today, when one visits along the relocated County Road #2, one can still see traces of our old villages. The road that used to cross our village by the water now ends in the water and appears on the other shore, while our village has been submerged.

We were indeed here!

A Straight Line of Trees

A straight line of trees and a water pump are but a few giveaway traces of the landscape which are witnesses of another era. They are the last vestiges of a family's former home setting facing the distant river.

Families had to make important decisions about their homes: leave them behind to be destroyed before the flood; relocate them in a new community or a place of their choice; accept monetary compensation for land and home; or, move one's family somewhere else. The choice to move or not to move was not an option. Everyone had to go.

It was a challenge beyond what human imagination had anticipated. Considering that quiet villages had settled into a relatively comfortable and predictable stability over the years, the pioneering spirit and sense of survival were greatly challenged.

While for a large number of families the move was devastating emotionally, socially, and economically, others welcomed the opportunity, preferring to believe in what the future might bring. The days, the months, and the years ahead might bring prosperity and a better life. Indeed, a good number of families and enterprises did well during the construction of the project and continued to prosper after 1958.

At the beginning of the project, in August 1954, while unsettled feelings were permeating the communities, families were starting to make plans for their future. Discussions relative to the enlargement of the St. Lawrence River, the creation of a new hydro electric powerhouse, the building of structures necessary for expanded navigation, and the probable relocation of homes, which had been the foci of the families' attention for the last fifty years, were becoming reality.

The objective of the plan, which was started on August 10, 1954, was to move people, families, homes, and expropriate land to make way for the implementation of the Seaway and Power project. Indeed, communities were presented with plans, blueprints, and models which outlined the relocation of six thousand five hundred people, five hundred thirty homes, six entire villages, two partial villages, three hamlets, more than two hundred twenty farms, eighteen cemeteries, thirty-one miles (50 km) of County Road #2, and forty-six and a half miles (72 km) of railroad. Over twenty-two thousand acres of land were necessary for the construction of a power generation dam in Cornwall, the creation of a head-pond to support the hydro electric generators, and other structures required by the new navigational channel and power project.

From its approval to the opening of the floodgates of the gigantic seaway, to the inundation of the St. Lawrence River, the project would spread over four years.

There would be another five years of restoration to be done after the flood.

The St. Lawrence River Prior to 1954

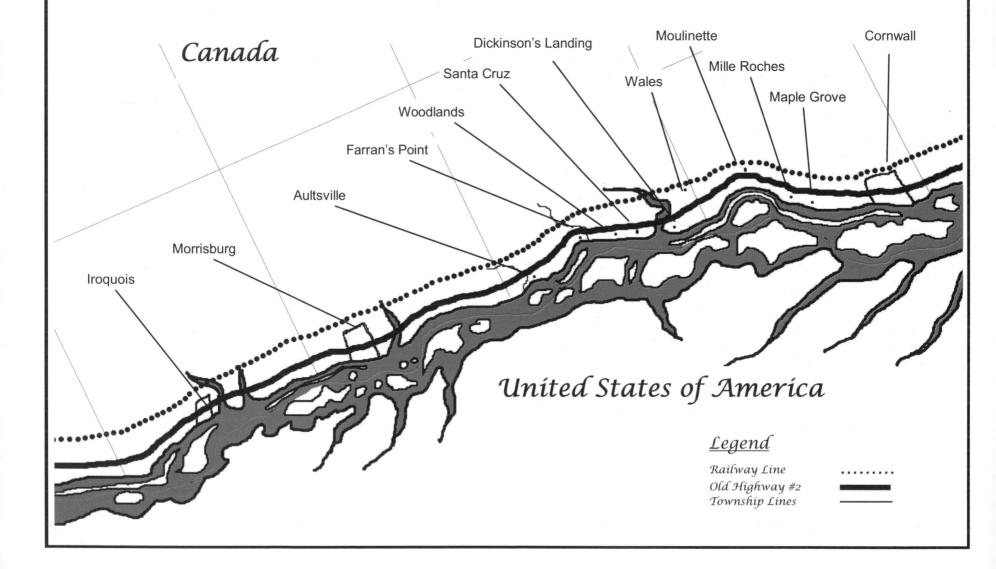

Canada

United States of America

Iroquois
Morrisburg
Aultsville
Farran's Point
Woodlands
Santa Cruz
Dickinson's Landing
Wales
Moulinette
Mille Roches
Maple Grove
Cornwall

135 Years of Geography

The geography of the St. Lawrence River was born ten thousand years ago when the glaciers of the last ice age advanced and retreated to leave behind material of glacial and marine origin. Having the density of concrete, the glacial till makes a good part of the soil along the St. Lawrence River. The bedrock from Montreal to the Thousand Islands is composed of shales, sandstone, limestone, dolomite, and granite.

Ever since the first voyageurs embarked on the fur trade, from the Lachine Rapids through the Long Sault Rapids to the Great Lakes, the St. Lawrence River proved to be a very difficult waterway for navigation. Although the flow of the water from the Great Lakes was considered constant at 246,000 cubic feet/second (6982.4 cubic m/sec) along its way, the depth of the St. Lawrence was greatly uneven. The river was rocky, treacherous, and tortuous. The water level from Lake Erie to Lake Ontario dropped three hundred twenty-six feet (99.4 m). Between Lake Ontario and Montreal, referred to as the International Rapids section, the river dropped ninety-two feet(28 m), another eighty-two feet (24.9 m) at Soulanges-Beauharnois, and fifty feet (15.2 m) at Lachine for a total of five hundred fifty feet (167.6 m).

In addition, there were a number of rapids to avoid. From Iroquois to Cornwall there were the Galops rapids, the Rapids Plat at Morrisburg, the Farran's Point rapids, and the Long Sault rapids. The St. Lawrence River also varied in width from a few miles wide (over 3 km) to a few hundred miles (over 160 km) wide in the Great Lakes sections. Indeed, the International Rapids section spread over forty-four miles (70 km) on the St. Lawrence River between Iroquois and Cornwall, and across two counties, Dundas, west of Aultsville, and Stormont on the east. Moreover, as the ice receded, the flood waters from the Great Lakes forced Point Iroquois to partly separate from the mainland whilst maintaining its proximity to the American shores.

The counties of Stormont and Dundas are located at the 45th parallel of latitude, i.e. half-way between the North Pole and the Equator. Considering that the St. Lawrence River is situated, in part, between Canada and the United States of America, an existing international line divided the Canadian and the American waters. Rapids were situated on either side of the boundaries of the international waters.

Along this area of the river, a number of islands, shoals, and small bays had been carved out by the water over centuries. Some islands had been the object of settlement within treaties between the two countries since the war of 1812. Sheek's Island and Cornwall Island were the largest amongst a number of small Canadian islands. Other large islands such as Long Sault Island, Barnhart Island, and Croil's Island were within American territory. Considering that the forest was lush and that the land possessed a rich soil in which to develop good agriculture, the banks of the St. Lawrence River were fertile ground for good farming. Moreover, there were a number of creeks, emptying into the St. Lawrence River, which had served to provide water power for the numerous mills constructed along the banks.

The St. Lawrence Seaway and Power Project represented 135 years of work from the construction of the first canals in 1824, to an internationally navigable Canadian waterway from the Great Lakes to the Atlantic Ocean, in 1959.

The geography of the St. Lawrence River would prove to be a significant challenge for the Ontario Hydro engineers who had to find ways to transform this great and powerful river into a navigable waterway and power-producing giant. The challenge was to alter its course for improved navigation, and to dam it strategically for the production of electrical energy. Channel improvement work was designed to remove natural barriers in the St. Lawrence River and to straighten its wandering course. Hydro electric power required the construction of a number of dams and power houses, on each side of the American and Canadian shores, to form a pool which would harvest the river's energy-giving capability.

The completion of the project would only happen when entire displaced communities could find other homes.

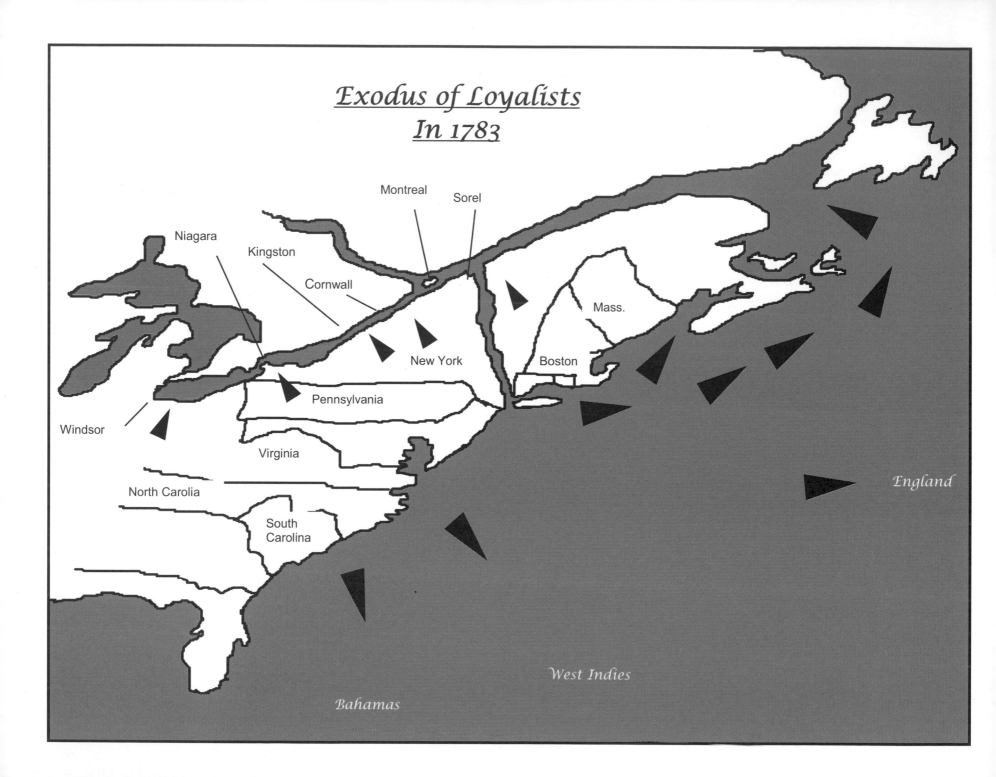

Exodus of Loyalists
In 1783

Niagara

Kingston

Montreal

Sorel

Cornwall

Mass.

New York

Boston

Windsor

Pennsylvania

Virginia

North Carolia

South
Carolina

England

West Indies

Bahamas

185 Years of History - Early Pioneers

The St. Lawrence River from Cornwall to Iroquois has a long history written, in part, by the presence of the native Indians over centuries, by the arrival of the French settlers in the 17th century, and further expanded by a wave of immigrants at the turn of the 18th century. The native Indians lived along the river and spread throughout this vast land. They developed a large network of forest pathways and trails, settled on the land, and lived off its resources.

The St. Lawrence River history is also written by the first French explorers who arrived on its shores, and, as early as 1680, created trading relationships with the various Indian tribes. The favoured means of transport of people, potash, grain, and other precious cargo down river to Montreal and back was by French batteaux, Durham boats, and rafts. Following the Plains of Abraham battle fought between French General Montcalm and British General Wolfe, the French Province of Quebec became British territory. Moreover, prior to the Imperial Statute passed in 1791, the territory of Canada was the land west of, and including, the British Province of Quebec.

Much of the history of the St. Lawrence River is also determined by its geography. At the end of the American Revolution and War of Independence, in 1783, the citizens who chose to fight against their country of adoption in support of the British Crown, found themselves without a country. As the country was no longer British land, by many, they were considered traitors. Moreover, as they were obliged to leave their American land, the waterway offered an escape route. Some Loyalists went back to the mother country, some to the southern West Indies and the Bahamas, and some to Nova Scotia. More travelled over land through Upper New York while others went north along the rivers, through Sorel and Montreal toward Cornwall, to the British Old Province of Quebec (later divided into Lower and Upper Canada) along the shores of the St. Lawrence River.

The land north of New York, Pennsylvania, and Massachusetts opened onto rich and fertile land, lush forest, and water power to develop mills. Thus, British Canada became a refuge for some seven thousand five hundred settlers made up of soldiers and their families. These servicemen either fought within the Royal Highland Emigrants or the King's Royal Regiment of New York. They had sacrificed what was most important to them - their homes - in defence of the British Crown under King George III and lost all personal possessions.

The approximately two thousand Iroquois Indians, from the Mohawk Valley in New York, settled on the south shore of the St. Lawrence River at St. Regis Island. Other immigrants, although in smaller numbers, were those who fled due to religious persecution, some black slaves who found new freedom, and those few in search of a new land to settle upon. Therefore 185 years of history span from 1774, beginning of the American War of Independence to 1959, year of the opening of the Seaway and Power project.

Families sought to live near one another for support and co-operation in farming activities necessary for survival. Moreover, soldiers, who had fought together, wished to remain together in the event of the necessity to defend their new land. Families sought self-sufficiency, supported the barter economy, and continued farming, thus gradually transforming the land into a means of support. In addition, mills of many kinds sprang up along the creeks and at the junctions of the river. Mills meant income, food, and improved economy.

Families faced formidable obstacles in their efforts to settle on their new land. They were surrounded by dangers of all kinds. Roaming wolves caused damage to farms and spread fear amongst farmers. Moreover, the forest was dense, the soil was rocky, the weather was severe, and the implements were limited. As roads were built and river traffic grew, small settlements appeared along the river.

The first home, near the river as it provided water for food and power for mills, was an eight by ten foot (2.4 m x 3.7 m) single-room shanty with its roof sloping at the back and with a cooking fireplace. Built of round logs, this temporary shelter included essential household necessities.

Architectural Styles

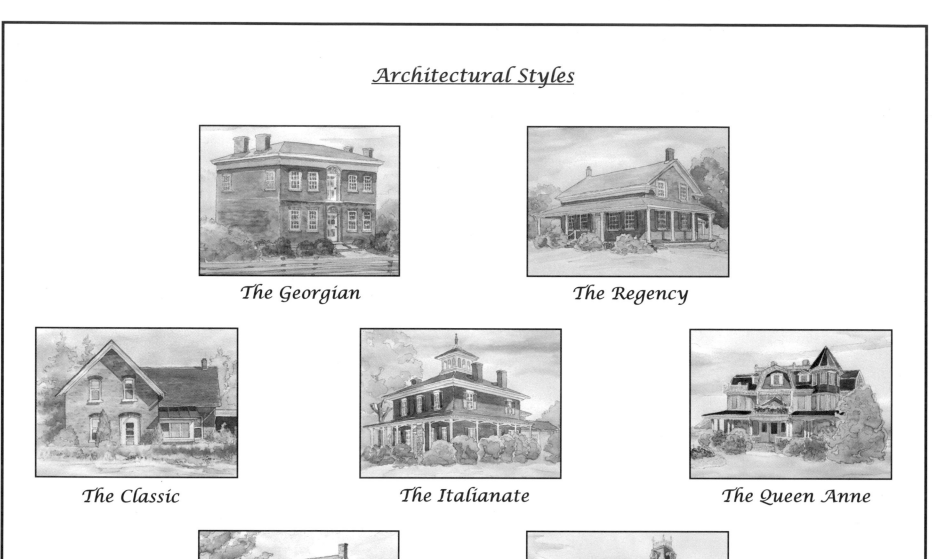

The Georgian

The Regency

The Classic

The Italianate

The Queen Anne

The Gothic

The Victorian

185 Years of History - The United Empire Loyalists

Those early settlers were called the United Empire Loyalists (UEL) on the basis of their allegiance to the British Crown. By Order-in-council, passed in 1789, it was announced that those soldiers, who had been loyal to the British Crown during the War of Independence, be assigned the distinguishing title of "UE" meaning Unity of the Empire. It was further declared that the title be given to every son and daughter of a Loyalist and that they be granted land as recognition of their service to the British King, George III. On their way to their new land, the Loyalists travelled through the wilderness with very few possessions to reach the Government depots either at Sorel, Chambly, or Cornwall. Once assigned lands, as per their location tickets, the refugees began the task of building new communities for themselves.

Prior to 1787, British land was organized into townships. The townships were seigneuries with the Government in Quebec City acting as landlord for the British King. The Loyalists petitioned for self government and a separate British province. It was, indeed, from pressure from the Loyalists that the Constitutional Act, passed on December 31st, 1791, divided the British Province of Quebec into Upper Canada (Ontario) and Lower Canada (Quebec). Furthermore, on June 16, 1792, the Lieutenant-Governor of Upper Canada, John Graves Simcoe, issued a proclamation declaring the Province of Upper Canada be divided into counties. The District of Lunenburg (named after Lunenburg, a district of Hanover, Germany) became the Eastern District comprising Glengarry, Stormont, and Dundas Counties. By 1812, the population of Upper Canada had grown to one hundred thousand. In 1850, all districts were abolished while the Eastern District became, to this day, the United Counties of Stormont, Dundas, and Glengarry. In 1867, under the Canadian Confederation Act, the Eastern provinces joined forces to create the new Canada. Upper Canada was renamed the Province of Ontario (meaning Shining Waters).

Most of the settlers landed in the various Townships of Glengarry, Stormont, and Dundas. Some of the settlers in Stormont and Dundas counties were Loyalists of German descent. They settled in the Townships of Osnabruck (named after a town in the province in Hanover, Germany), Williamsburg (named in 1787 in honour of Prince William Henry), and Matilda (named, in 1787, in honour of Charlotte Auguste Matilda, eldest daughter of George III), facing the St. Lawrence River. As this operation was a military re-settlement, and the settlers remembered "old country" differences, the Government believed that it was best to minimize frictions. Therefore, the Catholic Scotts were placed between the French Catholics in the east, and the Protestants in the west, in the area of Glengarry (named after Glen Garry of Inverness, Scotland). Dutch, Huguenot French, English, and Irish families moved further west in the counties of Stormont (named after David Murray, 7th Viscount Stormont, 1727-1796) and Dundas (named after the Right Honourable Henry Dundas, Treasurer of the British Navy from 1783 to 1801 and politician). Other immigrants to the county of Dundas were the German Lutherans of Palatine descent. It can, thus, be said that a large portion of the pioneers of Upper Canada and the land west were United Empire Loyalists.

Some of the basic architectural styles which they brought are deeply rooted in their personal ancestry, and styles developed in France, Britain, and the United States during the eighteenth and nineteenth centuries. Prior to 1820, the Loyalists introduced the Georgian style home with symmetrical facades, chimneys at each end of a medium-pitched gable or hip roof, and rectangular window openings. The Loyalist, a vernacular design, evolved as an adaptation of the Georgian home.

It was later (1810-1830) modified into a Regency home and included curves, such as the semi-elliptical transoms, emphasizing front doors. The one and a half storey Regency home style, developed in Britain between 1810 and 1840, has tall windows with many small panes of glass, wide chimneys, low hip or high-pitched roof, and various verandas. The later Revival styles - Classic, Renaissance, Gothic, Italianate, and Second Empire or Victorian, and Queen Anne produced larger and more elaborate homes with mansard and hip gable roofs, arched windows, and ornate brackets on eaves and verandas. Rectangular or square floor plans were less common. Moreover, homes showed regional and local adaptations as well as vernacular derivatives of the various styles.

Starting Over

Prior to 1791, date of the creation of the Province of Upper Canada, land grants were issued by Order-in-Council in the British Province of Quebec still under a Seigneurial system. Fearing that their grant under seigneurial tenure would make then tenants on their land, a number of Loyalists waited until the new Upper Canada came to be before claiming their land grants. Therefore, from 1792 until 1830, the land grants were issued under the British Province of Upper Canada giving them full ownership. While a number of conditions were attached to the grants of land, families who received grants agreed, as a first condition, to build a dwelling on the land within a year and to develop the land in the succeeding years.

Sir Frederick Haldiman, Governor of Quebec, was instrumental in the smooth re-settlement of the Loyalists. He had estimated that to re-settle 5,251 people, twenty-one seigneuries would be required for a total of 483,840 acres of land. It included the region from the Bay of Quinte in the west to Lake St-Francis in the east. In 1783, in preparation for the arrival of the Loyalists, Patrick McNiff had surveyed and divided the land to be settled along the St. Lawrence River into concessions and lots. The work had been done under the direction of Sir John Johnson, who was responsible for the soldiers who had fought in the War of Independence. Concessions and lots were numbered from south to north and east to west respectively. At the time, surveyor's instruments were called " chains". A chain was made up of one hundred links of equal length for a total length of sixty-six feet (20 m), when extended. A full lot, made of 20 chains in width and a greater depth, measured two hundred acres. An allowance was made for a road while a strip between the fifth or sixth lot was left for a cross road.

Upon arrival in 1784, the immigrants drew lots to determine their lands. Field officers received five thousand acres, captains received three thousand acres, lieutenants five hundred acres, and privates two hundred acres with land reserved in the back concessions for their children when they became of age. Many soldiers, who had fought together, wished to live close to each other as a means of support for the challenging life ahead. Thus, some families exchanged lots to be closer to each other and friends. The majority of new arrivals were farmers, cheese makers, carpenters, blacksmiths, shoemakers,

plumbers, bakers, and clay and pottery makers. With a meager allotment of provisions (one cow for two families, an axe and few other necessary tools and equipment) which the British Government had supplied them, farmers faced the next years struggling to transform the dense forests into farms and the river into an accessible water route. Working the land was hard labour. Developing the river as a source of transport and business required creativity and ingenuity.

To support the family, wool mills and grist and lumber mills were built along the river. Life for the immigrant pioneers was most challenging. Winter and summer, they worked hard to develop new communities along the St. Lawrence River. They transformed their new forest and new land into farms, villages, indeed, new communities. They tamed the river and used it to bring prosperity to their burgeoning communities.

The pioneer's first temporary single-roomed shanty, built of round pine or basswood logs, was soon replaced by another larger one also built of logs notched at the corners and chinked. The roof was made of elm bark, with one four-pane-window, a door, and a fireplace built of stone. The chimney was very often entirely made of stone. As the family grew, the new immigrant expanded his home into a farming complex. The log house would be used as a poultry house or piggery. The frame dwelling constructed from sawn or hewn wood with two to three-inch (5 to 8 cm) planks soon replaced the log cabin.

The MacLeod home is a good example of an original log home. Once on the property of Norman MacLeod, in1982, thanks to the generosity of Donald MacLeod and Lionel Grant, the home was moved by Rolland MacDonald to Ault Park, site of the Lost Villages Museum and Historical Society. As the first building moved to the Museum, it houses a number of historical artifacts and is often used as a resource centre.

The shanty dwelling and barn are added as a representation of what a farm complex might have looked like.

The Canals on the St. Lawrence River

Although the seventeenth century coureurs-des-bois and other fur-traders used the St. Lawrence River to gain access to the Canadian interior, the geography proved most inadequate for eighteenth and nineteenth century general travel, for more extensive trading of goods, and for military requirements. The transporting of fur, lumber, and wheat to the growing European markets was becoming increasingly difficult. Moreover, tension between the Americans and the British made improved river transport a military necessity. As roads were practically non-existent, the river was seen as the expedient method for travel and for shipping.

From 1779 to 1783, under the direction of Governor Sir Frederick Haldimand, the first two-and-a-half-foot (.7 m) canal system was built. In 1845, it was followed by a new series of seven- to nine-foot (2.1 to 2.7 m) canals. The Lachine Canal, the first one to be built in 1824, allowed boats to detour the rapids around the Island of Montreal. It was followed by a number of other canals built by William and Andrew Elliott on the borders of the towns of Cornwall upstream to Iroquois.

The Cornwall Canal, eleven and a quarter miles (18 km) long, was built from Cornwall to east of Dickinson's Landing. The other canals belonged to the Williamsburg Canal system. They were the three-quarters of a mile (1.2 km) long canal at Farran's Point, the four-mile (6 km) Rapids Plat Canal at Morrisburg, and the five-mile (9 km) Galops Canal which severed Point Iroquois and the mainland. Later the Rapids Plat and Galop canals were joined as one longer navigational passage. The canal walls, a tribute to the work of Scottish masons brought in to build the Rideau canal north of Kingston, were made of quarried limestone rocks placed in rip-rap fashion. The canal locks allowed vessels to move upstream or downstream smoothly by changing water levels within a lock chamber.

Canoes, French batteaux, and Durham boats were the original means of transport. The French batteau was long and narrow - forty to fifty feet (12 to 15 m) long, with a beam of five to eight feet (1.5 to 2.5 m) and had a pointed bow and stern. It could carry up to four and a half tons (4,091 kg)

of goods and required approximately a dozen crew members. Somewhat cumbersome, it was adaptable to a wide range of weather conditions and was able to manoeuver along a difficult river route. On the other hand, the Durham boat, used at the end of the eighteenth century, was a flat bottom boat. Of American origin and inspired from the "batteau", it was larger in size, measuring eighty to ninety feet (24.4 to 27.4 m), and was able to carry five times the batteaux's cargo of goods. Its bow was rounded, and it had a rudder at its stern end.

Both the batteaux and the Durham boats met competition when the canallers and the steam boats made their appearance during the first quarter of the nineteenth century. The canallers were known as the "two hundreds" as they measured two hundred sixty feet (79 m) long with a beam of fifty feet (15 m) and a draft of seven feet (2.1 m). They transported grain and lumber and managed the canals at speeds of up to ten knots. From 1845 on, vessels with a draft up to nine feet (2.7 m), carrying pulpwood and other commodities, could more easily manoeuver the St. Lawrence River between Montreal through Cornwall to Iroquois.

On land parallel to the canal, and along tow paths, oxen and horses were used to pull small boats up river. By the time the Cornwall Canal was completed in the 1850s, travel from the west continued to be possible, but from the east it had been considerably facilitated. The need to disembark people and goods to continue the trip by coach was no longer required. Coming down the river with people, grain, and other commodities from the farmland became a one day affair.

The canals continued to be widened and dredged even deeper between navigable waterways until 1904 when the fourteen-foot (4.3 m) canal became a reality. Moreover, with the introduction of the steamboat, travel became more enjoyable and the transport of goods was made more efficient and less costly. Occasionally, steamships, with sightseers, would "shoot the rapids" instead of using the canals and lock system. By 1954, the old canals and lock system had become obsolete.

The Seaway Project

From 1680 on, there were dreams of opening the river from the Great Lakes to the Atlantic Ocean. There were hopes of bringing missionaries, fur trappers, and pioneers to the new world and bringing back lumber, minerals, grains, furs, and other goods. At the turn of the twentieth century, it was believed that a more efficient way had to be found to allow heavier sea-going vessels, with drafts of more than fourteen feet (4.3 m), access to inland ports. Harnessing the great waterpower of the St. Lawrence River to produce kilowatts of electricity which would support the growing industries along the river was the object of discussion on both sides of the river. Moreover, the rapids, although obstacles to navigation, had hydro electric potential which could be used to benefit the increased need for energy.

The Seaway and Power Project became a reality four hundred years after Jacques Cartier, the European explorer, named the great river Saint Lawrence, the patron saint of the day. In 1906, the Ontario Hydro Electric Commission was founded. It was followed by the development of a provincial board set up to study the hydroelectric capacity of the St. Lawrence River. After a number of years of engineering studies, in March 1925, the American and the Canadian governments created a joint board of engineers with the mandate to develop a comprehensive plan for the development of the river for navigation and power. In fact, discussions relative to a seaway-power project initiated at the turn of the century did not come to fruition until 1951.

Future international joint use of the river for navigation and power required that the project planning, construction, and operation be coordinated by the two bordering countries. Therefore, combined with the needs for increased electricity and the expansion of the St. Lawrence River for navigation, the Canadian and the American governments approved the project. In partnership, the Ontario Hydro Electric Commission and the Power Authority of the State of New York, with the help of the supportive legislation from both countries, announced on July 13, 1954, that the "Seaway and Power Project" was born. Furthermore, on August 10, 1954, the sod-turning ceremonies held concurrently in Cornwall and Massena, New York, marked the official beginning of the project. The International Rapids section of the river was subsequently re-named the Seaway Valley.

The Seaway aspect of the project consisted of modifying the infrastructure required for improved navigation by building a new forty mile (64 km) canal with a series of seven locks, replacing a forty-seven mile (75 km) canal system with locks, from Lake Ontario to the Gulf of St. Lawrence. From west of Iroquois, at Galop Island to Cornwall, the channel was dredged to a depth of twenty-seven feet (8 m) and the bridges were either reconfigured or rebuilt entirely to create a continuous passage for vessels. Two new bridges were built, the International Bridge, in Cornwall and the Champlain bridge, in Montreal, while the Jacques Cartier bridge, also in Montreal, was raised. The navigation channel which starts at the Iroquois lock extends through Lake St. Lawrence. It continues to the Wiley-Dondero shipping channel, in the United States, with its twin forty-five-foot (13.7 m) locks, the Dwight D. Eisenhower and the Bertrand H. Snell, built to overcome an eighty-seven foot (26 m) fall at the Moses-Saunders powerhouse.

Navigation was never interrupted during construction. Vessels used the old canals and locks to avoid strong currents. Preliminary work started conjointly at the Cornwall powerhouse and at the Iroquois site in 1955. The Iroquois lock is eight hundred sixty feet (262 m) long by eighty feet (24.4 m) wide and has a six-foot (1.8 m) lift. It features a lift bridge modeled on the medieval drawbridge. The two American locks, situated along the seven-mile Wiley-Dondero channel, are equipped with miter gates, while the Iroquois lock has sector-type gates. The tip of Iroquois Point was removed to improve the flow of the river through the dam. Moreover, Iroquois Point, which was bisected by the Seaway project, now stands south of the new channel and locks.

Since that day, on August 10, 1954, the lives of the riverside communities, as well as the shores of the St. Lawrence River, were changed forever.

As riverside communities, rare were the villagers who could not see the river from their windows, hear the river, keep an eye out for river activities, indeed, feel the pulse of the river.

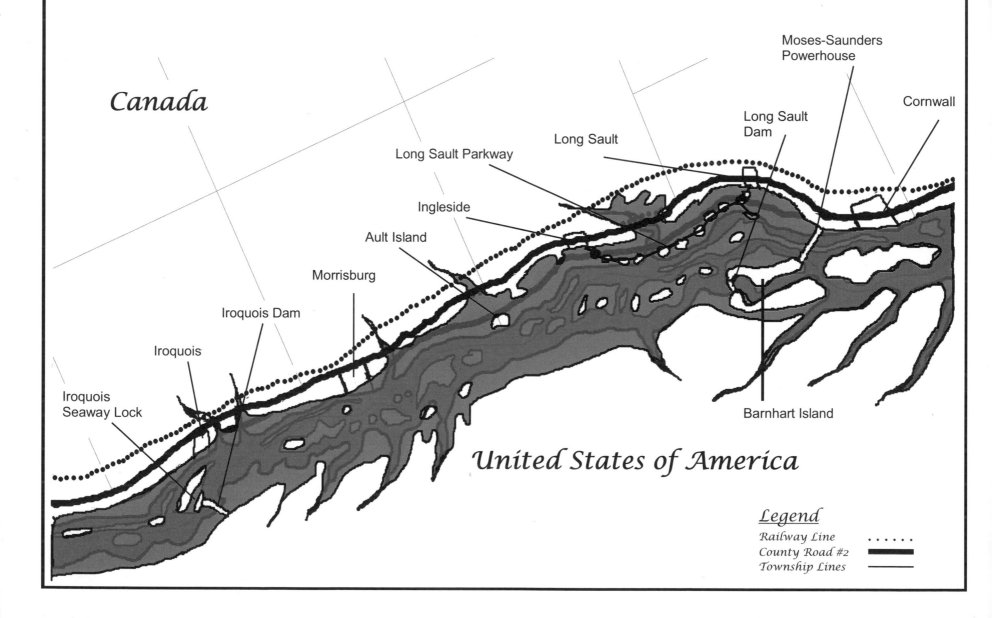

The St. Lawrence River After 1958

Moses-Saunders
Powerhouse

Canada

Cornwall

Long Sault
Dam

Long Sault

Long Sault Parkway

Ingleside

Ault Island

Morrisburg

Iroquois Dam

Iroquois

Iroquois
Seaway Lock

Barnhart Island

United States of America

Legend
Railway Line · · · · · ·
County Road #2 ▬▬▬
Township Lines ——

The Power Project

Parallel with the opening of the waterway to seagoing vessels, the need for increased power, in both countries, was seen as a means to improve the region economically and to open it to world markets. Indeed, it was foreseen that some seaway communities would turn into international seaports. Closely interconnected with the Seaway project, the large-scale hydro electric Power project was undertaken by Ontario Hydro and the Power Authority of the State of New York in the International section of the river. The objective was to use the power offered by the river's constant flow of 246,000 cubic feet/sec (6982.4 cubic m/sec), and the drop in water levels between the eastern end of Lake Ontario and Cornwall, to its advantage.

Three structures were needed for harnessing the power of the river. The network of dams had to be changed to create two new dams, while a new power generation plant had to be built across the Canadian-American borders. They were the Iroquois and the Long Sault dams, and the Moses-Saunders Powerhouse, in Cornwall.

The project started at the Iroquois dam and the Cornwall powerhouses. The dam, a buttressed gravity structure which spans 2,540 feet (746.8 m) between Point Iroquois in Canada, and Point Rockaway in the United States, was built to control the flow of the river between Iroquois and Cornwall. The Long Sault dam, a gravity spillway structure with lift gates, three miles (4.8 km) west of the Moses-Saunders Powerhouse, controls the depth of the power pool and the water level behind the powerhouse. The Long Sault dam measures 2,250 feet (685.8 m) long spanning Barnhart Island, in Canada, and the American mainland. The building of the dams required that both north and south sections of the river in turn be dried up temporarily. Coffer dams and diversion canals were used to redirect the water, alternatively north and south.

The International boundary of the St. Lawrence River was re-drawn to include powerhouses in both countries. The Cornwall power generation plant was built two miles (3.2 km) west of Cornwall, between Cornwall and Barnhard Island. It measures 3,000 feet (914.4 m) in length, 150 feet (45.7 m) high and houses 32 generators shared equally between the two countries (16 Canadian, 16 American) producing 1,800 megawatts of electricity. Dykes and embankments were built to confine the Lake St. Lawrence water level which was higher than the surrounding countryside.

Models of the river, replicating its entire length and simulating various conditions, were built. The study of the flow of the river and its impact on the future structures would improve precision of the work and provide answers which, it was found, would eventually save millions of dollars. Winter time was especially challenging to men and machines. The earth, made of glacial till, when mixed with rocks had the density of concrete. It was wet, sticky, and clung like glue to machines and equipment. "The Gentleman", a huge machine brought in from Kentucky, USA, had the task of chewing into the soil for the excavation of the new channel. Field offices, men, shovels, bulldozers, explosives, and other heavy equipment appeared on the landscape.

While the Canadian hydro electric powerhouse was named Robert Saunders, in honour of the late chairman of Ontario Hydro who had been instrumental in bringing it into reality, the American one was named Robert Moses, in honour of the chairman of the New York Power Authority. The newly created lake for improved navigation, thirty-five miles (56 km) long by three miles (5 km) wide, between the Iroquois and the Long Sault dams, would also serve as a head pond for the Robert Saunders-Robert Moses power generating plant. It was named Lake St. Lawrence.

The project spanned over four years, with an additional five years to finalize all settlements and required 500 engineers, 22,000 construction workers, at a cost of $400,000,000 for the Seaway project and $600,000,000 for the entire International Power Project.

Water Obstacles

The most famous and challenging of water obstacles which had to be overcome was the majestic Long Sault Rapids. The rapids extended one and a half mile (2.4 km) between the east end of Long Sault Island and the western end of Sheek's Island. Considering the rapid flow of the river south of Long Sault Island, and its drop of forty feet (12.2 meters) in a short distance, regular shipping by-passed the rapids. Boats used the fourteen-foot (4.3 meters) Cornwall Canal. Some of the most adventurous residents and visitors enjoyed "running the rapids", that is, boating down the river over the rapids on such excursion steamers as the "Rapids King", "Rapids Queen", and the "Rapids Prince". These turbulent waters had provided long and enjoyable hours of recreation for residents. Sunday afternoon picnics, swimming, summer canoeing, boating, and camping were some of the very popular activities enjoyed near the rapids. Their fascinating power had attracted thousands of tourists who spent numerous weekends and summer holidays near the rough waters. Artists and painters appreciated their natural and rugged beauty.

Another major water obstacle explorers and navigators had faced over the centuries had been the numerous other rapids along the St. Lawrence River between Iroquois and Cornwall. Traveling on the river had been greatly challenged by the various detours and circumvolutions canoes, batteaux, and steam boats had to make to avoid its dangers. Transportation of goods had been further complicated by the unpredictable irregularity of the shallow waters. Their shores had been the sites of smaller summer camps, beaches, swimming wharves, and boating ramps set up to provide easy access to the river. The old familiar canals with their supporting locks built to avoid the rapids, their power houses and light houses, which had served the communities well over a century and a half, had to be destroyed.

The construction of the power dams required that the Long Sault rapids be drained for a period of a few months. While the coffer dams held the waters back, it was observed that over centuries the rushing waters of the Long Sault rapids had formed a bedrock of interesting shapes.

Cannon balls dropped off a ship, years ago, were some of the treasures found on the dry river bed. Along with the Long Sault rapids, the traces of history left behind, over centuries, from Iroquois to Cornwall were eliminated.

The constant water flow of the river and its tributaries, as well as its undeniable power, had been tapped over the last two centuries to feed the numerous mills which had sprouted along the river in the local villages. Mills had provided a constant source of income and had supported a variety of trades for the growing pioneer villages. Bergin Lake, west of Cornwall, resulted from the construction of the original canals and dams. It had been named in honour of Dr. Darby Bergin (1826-1896), who had served the community as a medical practitioner, a Member of Parliament for Cornwall Township, and in 1861, had been placed in charge of a company of militia. In 1869, Colonel Darby Bergin took over the responsibility for the old 59th Stormont and Glengarry Battalion. In 1958, Bergin Lake had to go.

Other obstacles which had been extensively studied by a Canadian-American joint board of engineers during the first quarter of the twentieth century were the composition of the river bed materials and their ability to support the construction of dams as well as that of temporary coffer dams. Flooding consequences, according to different water elevations for various discharges of volumes of water during winter seasons, were also studied. Conclusive research found the river able to support the demands of the project. Thus, the old river and its past features were changed to make way for the new river and its new structures.

In 1958, at the end of the construction, when the waters flooded the land, it also flooded the old river with its historic Long Sault rapids, its old canals, Bergin lake, and its old dams.

They disappeared under more than seventy feet (21.3 m) of water.

Land Obstacles

The St. Lawrence River from Cornwall to Iroquois would be flooded to an elevation of two hundred forty-two feet (73.8 m) above sea level. In order for the Seaway and the Power Project to be implemented, land obstacles had to be overcome. These would cause safety issues. Homes, cemeteries, churches, schools, entire villages, historic landmarks and sites, as well as other community buildings, had to be removed or destroyed.

All traces of the previous villages had to be eliminated before the creation of Lake St. Lawrence. As well, twenty-two thousand acres of farm and residential land in the counties of Stormont and Dundas, for a total of two thousand one hundred and ninety land acquisitions and two hundred twenty-five farms, were flooded.

Six thousand five hundred people, from Stormont and Dundas counties, were displaced and five hundred thirty homes were moved by Ontario Hydro, while some others were moved by their owners. It can be assumed that more than two thousand homes were destroyed by fire or bulldozers. Three hundred forty-nine new homes were built. In 1956, before the landscape would be changed permanently, it was with great interest that fourteen architecture students from the Ontario College of Art sketched and measured a number of homes. They worked under the supervision of Ruth Home, Director of the Museum Research Studies and Marian McRae doing a thesis research project.

Moreover, the flooding caused a number of islands to disappear completely while others partly survived. All twenty-nine cottages from Sheek's Island, partly flooded, were moved to Island 17 (Moulinette Island) south of the new town of Long Sault, and Ault Island along County Road # 2 (sometimes referred to as Highway #2) east of Upper Canada Village Museum.

In the Cornwall township, the villages of Moulinette and Mille Roches were completely submerged. In the township of Osnabruck, the entire villages of Dickinson's Landing, Wales, Farran's Point, and Aultsville, disappeared. The infrastructure of sidewalks, roads, much of the farmland situated inland along Hoople's Creek, with the hamlets of Santa Cruz, Woodlands, and Maple Grove were also lost. In the townships of Mathilda and Williamsburg respectively, the Old Iroquois was moved east and within the town boundaries, while some homes, as well as the business section of Morrisburg, were also relocated in an area created for the new community.

Three of twenty-three churches and eighteen cemeteries dating back to the eighteenth and nineteenth centuries from the old villages were relocated to new areas. Along with 5059 graves and 2560 headstones, fifteen historical sites were also relocated. The Maple Grove cemetery, situated on land deeded by Jeremiah French to the Trinity Anglican Church in 1804, with its three hundred seventeen graves and remains was moved to a new location along the Highway #2, west of Cornwall. All other cemeteries with selected remains were also moved to the Union cemetery along Highway #2, close to the site of the former village of Wales. The cemetery was divided into areas falling under the various local church jurisdictions. Families had the option either to have the remains of their loved ones disinterred and moved or to move only the markers, gravestones, or headstones. Remains left behind were covered with rocks and stones to ensure that they would be left undisturbed under water. Religious as well as cemetery representatives accompanied families during the re-burials.

The old Iroquois and Mille Roches Powerhouses erected in 1901 were also destroyed.

Three thousand six hundred acres of timber and eleven thousand trees were cut to eliminate possible water hazards. Today, on spring and fall days when the water of the St. Lawrence River is low, the tree trunks and sidewalks of the old villages can still be seen. Chopped tree trunks, a wharf, and weeds now lay where a family once lived.

The Masterman Home

The destruction of the environment included the destruction of the old Highway # 2 between Iroquois and Cornwall as well as forty double-track miles (64 km)of the Canadian National Railway lines. A new railway line and thirty-seven miles (59 km) of Highway #2 were relocated north of the new villages. A good stretch of the new County Road #2 was relocated above the two hundred and fifty foot (76.2 m) sea level watermark as a means to provide a buffer for possible fluctuations of water level.

The Masterman family home, more than one half mile (.8 km) from the river, in Wales, was situated between the St. Lawrence River and the Canadian Pacific railway bridge over Hoople's Creek.

Hoople's Creek meandered through farmland and met with the St. Lawrence River at Dickinson's Landing. The stone bridge over the creek was built as a part of the Canadian Railway network. Built by the English firm of Peto, Brassey, Jackson, and Betts, with the assistance of Civil Engineer Cazimir Gzowski, the Grand Trunk Railway connecting Portland, Maine, to Sarnia Ontario, was largely financed by British capital. Referred to as a 'main line', it was completed in the 1850s. The Pacific Railway built a line from Montreal to Toronto in the 1880s. In 1920, the Grand Trunk was taken over by the Federal Government Canadian National Railways.

Railway transportation was instrumental in the economic as well as the social lives of the communities. The train had served the communities along the St. Lawrence River from Montreal to Brockville since 1854. Commuters depended on the train to bring goods, services, and other amenities back and forth to their small communities. Travel to schools in Cornwall was facilitated by the train. For many years, travel by train from Iroquois to Ottawa required a transfer through Cornwall.

It had served much the same purpose as the canals did by providing portage routes for people, goods, and mail between two adjacent navigable waterways. Moreover, communities along the lines provided fire wood for the steam engine. However, with the arrival of diesel fuel, in the 1950s, the era of steam came to an end. The typically Canadian train, affectionately named "Mocassin", made its last run in August 1957. After 103 years of service, steam engine number 5280 ceased to operate and its steam whistle was silenced.

It was, indeed, with sadness and nostalgia, that people witnessed the disappearance of the "Mocassin". It had been named after the St-Regis Indians who wore mocassins. They used to raft logs to Montreal and travel to reed beds near Brockville and Kingston before returning home by train.

Only two finely restored train stations survived the implementation of the project. The Moulinette train station stands at Ault Park, the site of the Lost Villages Museum, in Long Sault, while the Aultsville train station has been moved west of Upper Canada Village Museum, in Morrisburg on a short track from its old rail bed. New stations were built to accommodate the relocated train lines. The new forty mile (64 km) double-track and spur lines required 19,300 tons (17513 m tons) of steel rails, with approximately one-half million tie plates, more than one-quarter million ties and over one million spikes to fasten the steel rails to the ties.

Although the Masterman home was destroyed, the railway bridge, which had recently been repaired with cement reinforcement under its arches, still stands today under the water of Lake St. Lawrence.

Thus, the first phase of the Seaway and Power project, named the "destruction", was completed when all traces of the old villages were erased and the flat, desolate, and treeless expanse of land waited to be flooded.

The Home by the St. Lawrence River

There were negotiations between every land, home, and business owner in the lost villages and Ontario Hydro. The value of each property had to be established. Homes, barns, farm buildings, arenas, public buildings, stores, churches, schools, and apple orchards, were assigned values. At the beginning of the project, in 1954, three options were given to land and business owners: monetary compensation of equal value; re-build the home and business in the new community; monetary compensation plus 10% to 15% allowance for the inconvenience or the disturbance caused by the needed move. A combination of the two previous offers was also possible.

Aware of the emotional reaction and possible opposition to the proposed displacement of families, and mandated to ensure success of the relocation, Ontario Hydro initially enlisted the support of many influential members of the communities among which were the leaders of the churches. The next steps were to explain the plans to the various local associations and offer support to the residents by initiating the formation of community-based advocacy groups.

A number of families chose the options offered. However, since the project had threatened the valley for some fifty years, the real estate was depressed. A climate of uncertainty was prevailing. Concerned with establishing fair compensation, and aware that land and property value had suffered depreciation, residents introduced the concept of replacement value rather than market value. Considering that replacing a modest home was not possible for less than ten thousand dollars in many cases, Ontario Hydro representatives were relieved when the residents of Iroquois suggested moving homes and their attached buildings, to the new communities. Thus, a fourth offer was made by Ontario Hydro which included moving homes from one site to another.

All homes were assigned numbers to assist in the move, to specify their status, and their destination. A number such as SL 494 (St. Lawrence) would indicate the home's origin, its destination, and certain considerations. Homes were classified into two categories: those homes which could be moved and those which could not be moved due to their size and construction.

Movable homes, purchased by Ontario Hydro, would be relocated in the new communities. They would be made available for purchase by those who had found themselves unable to have their homes moved or who chose to leave their old homes to be destroyed. On first-come first-serve basis, priority was given to owners of moved homes, or of new homes to be built, to choose their lots in their new community. Those villagers, who had rented properties in the old villages, could continue to rent in the few rental units Ontario Hydro built. They were the next group to choose lots and, at their expense, could have new homes built. They could even purchase a moved home. New homes had to be built within a limited time or the assigned lots would be sold back to Ontario Hydro. Homes which could be moved were either moved by their owners or by the Ontario Hydro moving contractor, the James William Hartshorne House Moving Company. Verandas, garages, barns, and attached buildings were used either to expand a moved home or to transform a new home.

In the case of a home which could not be moved, where the owner wished to keep the family homestead, a negociated amount was arrived at between Ontario Hydro and the owner, plus a 15% allowance granted to the owner. Other homes were destroyed by fire or bulldozer.

As the Seaway and Power project started at Cornwall and Iroquois simultaneously, the hamlet of Maple Grove and the village of Iroquois were the first communities to experience the relocation.

While homes were either gone, burned, or bulldozed, foundations were submerged, reminders of one's lost village. Trees were cut and the landscape was laid bare. Soon other villages would suffer the same fate before being completely re-settled.

The Smith Home

The Seaway and Power Project was well on its way when it started with the destruction of some homes. Homes as well as buildings which could not be moved, were either bulldozed, dynamited, and/or burned. Homes were burned quickly and violently. Shortly after the home had been set on fire, emitting greyish smoke from every window and every crack, the structure was transformed into an inferno of bright orange. Often all that was left of the timber home was a fireplace, a chimney, a few unburnt sticks, an eerie skeleton of bricks, and other structures to be destroyed later.

The Smith home from Moulinette, a two-storey brick building with a large front bay window, was sold to Ontario Hydro. After the family moved to Cornwall, the house was burned. It was originally owned by Dr. Harrison, who, it is thought, ran his medical practice from the home, followed by the Adams family and the Abbot family. Witnesses report that the home was just as beautiful inside as it was outside, with a mural on the curving staircase.

Ontario Hydro photographers were hired to document the entire Seaway and Power project. With Harry Wilson in charge, Carl Malcolm, John Phippen, and Charles Wilkins photographed the destruction and the construction in progress. Dams, old powerhouses, roads, and dwellings were photographed from all angles throughout the seasons and under various weather conditions during the four years of the project. They also photographed all buildings and homes which were affected before their relocation or their destruction. As all photographs were dated, they not only served to document all aspects of the project but also served to settle possible disagreements which may have arisen. They recorded possible building damage during the move, construction faults, or even the origin of a home or an attached building.

Photographs not only served to build archives, now the property of Ontario Hydro Corporation private collection, but were provided to the newspapers to increase understanding and support for the project. The collection was additionally expanded when, in 1960, the Corporation held its 7th annual Hydro Photographic Salon. Trophies, medals, and ribbons recognized winners in three categories - prints, nature slides, and pictorial slides.

In addition, using the given opportunity to undertake research, the National Research Council and the Government of Ontario conducted experiments on a number of houses and other buildings which were wired, set ablaze, and photographed. This research led to the development of smoke alarms. The Lost Village of Aultsville, where much research was done, became the "site of the burn", as it had been known.

One of the events that encapsulates the feeling of many residents at the time of the Seaway construction was told with a great deal of emotion by witnesses of a burning home. They were children in grade 3 who had been let out at morning recess. Unexpectedly, on that specific day, they witnessed a house burning - such as the Smith's home. "We will not forget the pain on our friend's face as well as the tears running down his cheeks when he realized that his own home was burning before his eyes." The feeling of being impotent in the face of adversity, when confronted with the loss of one's home as well as the shock of witnessing such destruction, left raw memories in those adults who remember their friend.

The archives have remained silent about the precise number of homes which were destroyed.

The Red Brick Home

It is not known who owned this red brick home at the time of the Seaway Project. However, it suffered the same fate as more than 2,000 other homes, ie., bought by Ontario Hydro, burned, and reduced to rubble by the bulldozers.

The destruction of a home by bulldozers was quite a visual experience. Long steel cables were used to destroy fine old farmhouses, churches, as well as barns and other buildings. Attached to the pulling machines, cables which had been inserted through the windows of the structure, ripped through the vertical posts holding up the first floor of the home. The bulldozers would then knock the corner supports before the building would start to shift and slowly fall to the ground, cracking under its own weight. Many of the homes were then burned.

The destruction not only applied to homes but to schools, to arenas, to stores, and to churches. Indeed, all but three churches from the villages west of Cornwall were destroyed. One church was moved to Upper Canada Village Museum and the other to the Riverside Heights community along the new County Road #2. The Anglican Christ Church from Moulinette was loaded on an Ontario Hydro flatbed by the William J. Hartshorne House Moving Company. In need of repair, after it was moved twenty-five miles (40 km) to its new destination on the grounds at Upper Canada Village Museum, it was refurbished.

The second church was the Trinity Anglican Memorial Church, also named the Whitney Memorial Church, from the riverside area of the St. Lawrence River, east of Morrisburg. Built in 1835 and renovated in 1902, it was dismantled completely to make way for the Seaway and rebuilt in the Riverside Heights community east of Morrisburg.

James P. Whitney, founder of Ontario Hydro Electric Power Commission was a Conservative Member of Parliament for Dundas from 1896 to 1905. Sir Whitney, born in Williamsburg in 1843, became the 6th Prime Minister of Ontario from 1905 to 1914, and was knighted in 1908. He died in New York on September 25, 1914, and is buried at the back of the cemetery. It is ironic to observe that Sir James Whitney's extensive support of the development of Ontario Hydro, as a public utility, caused the disappearance of his native riverside home situated west of Aultsville.

The third church, the Emmanuel Pentacostal Church, from Moulinette, was moved to Cornwall, eventually to become the Calvary Baptist Church, and eventually destroyed.

In the early communities, where clay was available, brickyards were set up. As bricks are not difficult to make, co-operative communities could produce a good quantity in a relatively short time. The Loyalists built their homes' exterior walls in two basic ways: they laid exterior bricks in various patterns, presenting different surfaces, held together with mortar, or they concealed bricks between the walls of a brick or wood frame home. Some intricate wall patterns included bricks laid in the Flemish bond style - every seventh row, the long side (stretcher) and the short side (header) of bricks alternated resulting in interesting details.

Quarried limestone, as a building material, was later used in the construction of homes. During the nineteenth century, as a means of defence against possible future invasion, skilled Scottish stone masons had built the Rideau Canal, south of Ottawa. When they became available, stone masons continued on to build homes in Upper Canada. Many elaborate homes of the late nineteenth century show a combination of intricate patterns of bricks decorated with elaborate masonry and stonework. The many courses of bricks and stones on the exterior walls of the nineteenth century homes tended to make them heavier than wood frame ones. Therefore, a large number of them were destroyed during the Seaway project construction.

The Rupert Home

Expropriation of the old villages and the displacement of their residents proved to be a challenge for a number of reasons. Some residents, who made associations with their past history and their attachment to the land of their ancestors, the United Empire Loyalists, going back two hundred years and more, experienced a great sense of loss. Others deplored the loss of farmland which could not be passed on to the next generation, while others felt great anxiety associated with moving away from their former homes. For others, the necessity to compensate for the loss of income, caused by the move, produced great turmoil.

As everyone had to go, the great house moving phase began.

House moving had been quite a sensation when it started during the summer of 1955. When the two Hartshorne "monster" machines arrived with the flat-bed trucks and other supporting equipment, residents knew the time had come for their homes to be moved. For the most part, furniture, dishes, and pictures would remain on the walls during the move. Electricity, plumbing, and other services were connected within a few days.

After the move was completed, heating, running water, and bathrooms were retrofitted to the homes needing to meet recently established standards. Minor repairs were made to the moved homes. A fresh coat of paint was given before owners took possession. Landscaping was done shortly afterwards. Hydro Ontario rehabilitation engineers were responsible for the cleaning and the inspection of the relocated home before a family took possession.

Some weeks prior to the chosen date, and after a move agreement was signed, the homeowner was notified of the moving plans. Ontario Hydro engineers, assisted with support staff, took necessary measurements of the home and its foundation. Ontario Hydro employees came over to clear the basement of the owners's possessions and place them in a temporary storage. On moving day, the family was accompanied to a stopover home, owned by Ontario Hydro, while the home was reset on its new foundation and adjustments were made. The stopover homes were equipped with all amenities needed for a temporary stay.

A family would usually reside at the stopover home from a few hours to a half-day. In the winter, the stay might extend to a few days, or up to two weeks while heating and water systems were hooked up. It has been reported that a stay of a year and longer was also possible.

Stopover homes were also used by residents who accepted compensatory payment for their homes sold to Ontario Hydro. Some residents, who had rented homes in the old villages, found themselves moving temporarily into stopover homes. Ontario Hydro used stopover homes for its staff of engineers who set up on-site offices, for supervisors and contractors, and for emergency and first aid centers.

The towns of Long Sault, Ingleside, Morrisburg, and Iroquois each had a number of stopover homes.

This stopover home, moved from Mille Roches to Long Sault, is one of twelve houses in the new communities of Long Sault and Ingleside, which was used as a stopover home. It was the property of Ralph Rupert and his family at the time of the Seaway project. Ontario Hydro, which bought the home from the family, transformed it into a stopover home.

It was during a friend's such stay-over that the present owners were "easily" persuaded to purchase the home, which they have enjoyed for years.

The Casselman Home

The last of five hundred thirty moved homes to escape the flooding was the Casselman Tudor style home from Morrisburg. It was built during the late 1930s, by Florence and Clinton Casselman. With its blend of half-timbered and stuccoed gable, the Tudor Queen Anne Revival style was a popular design during the first third of the twentieth century. The architecture, popular in Britain, was first established in Victoria, British Columbia.

Florence Casselman was the daughter of Alexander and Isabella Farlinger, and grand-daughter of United Empire Loyalist, Nicholas Farlinger, river captain, businessman, and banker. Together with her husband, Clinton, they raised two children in the home until the Seaway Project, when the family sold it to Ontario Hydro. The present owners purchased the home in 1960, and have lived in it ever since.

House moving was one of the more observed activities of the Seaway and Power project. Residents, visitors, and tourists were equally fascinated by the speed and efficiency with which homes were being relocated. The house moving phase of the Seaway and Power project started in Iroquois in June, 1955 and ended in Morrisburg in December, 1957.

Although some families moved their own homes, the Hartshorne House Moving Company, owned by Clarence and James William Hartshorne from Moorestown, New Jersey, moved five hundred thirty homes. The Company was responsible for the over-all move of homes and selected buildings along the thirty-five mile (56 km) area to be re-settled. Homes were moved on dirt roads, as far as a few miles (km) from their original communities, to their new destination. Some homes were lifted onto special flat-beds to be transferred to their new sites, while others were moved by the big machines. Roads were re-graded daily. Indeed, winter road conditions, including freezing and thawing, transformed unpaved surfaces into mud terrains.

The excavation engineers, the house moving engineers, the heating engineers, the building engineers, and the electrical engineers oversaw the general operations. On average, six homes a week were moved by the 'monster' machines. They could easily lift one hundred to two hundred-ton (91 to 181 m tons) homes with their ten-foot (3 m) high wheels and travel five miles per hour (8 km/hr). Some house roofs and peaks were removed prior to their meeting with Hydro wires on the road. The larger buildings, with summer kitchens, attached sheds, barns, and garages were transported in sections.

Prior to the move, the information officers met with the home owner to review the specific features of the move. To reassure home owners that the move would be safe, and that the home would arrive intact at its new destination, families were informed that they could leave dishes on the table and pictures on the walls.

After careful inspection, giant steel lifting beams projecting out from the foundation walls were bolted together to support the house during the move. The two Hartshorne moving machines could extend, in width, to accommodate any size home. Powered by drum winches, pulleys, and hooks, the long U-shaped extending arms of the moving rig lifted the home, transported it and deposited it approximately half a day or more later on a matching newly built concrete block foundation, at the new site. For the heaviest homes, the Hartshorne Company used steel dollies to carry them to their new destinations. The cost of moving a home ranged from one thousand to three thousand dollars.

Thirty-three months after it had started, when all buildings and homes had been moved, the big house moving operation came to an end.

In 1958, when all the work was completed, the water rose up to a depth of ninety feet (27 m) over the land. The flooding submerged the villages along the way.

These villages would be known as the Lost Villages of the St. Lawrence Seaway and Power project.

Part Two

« Lost Villages »

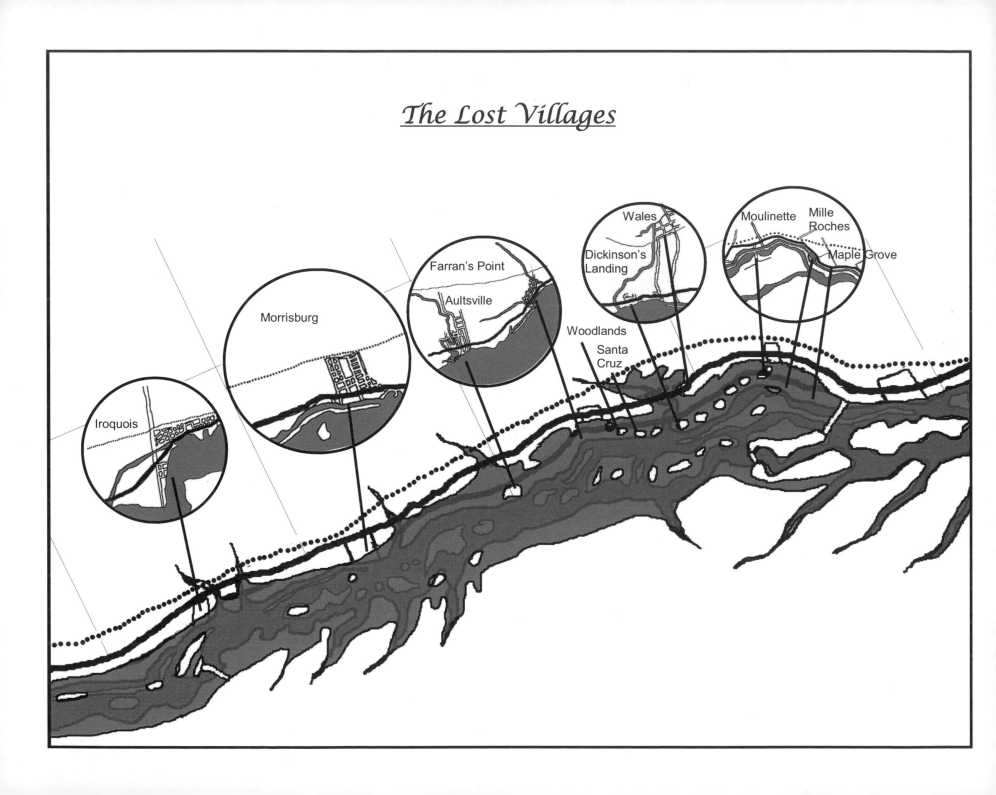

The Lost Villages

Inundation day, July 1st, 1958, as it was called, had arrived. When at 8 am. on July 1st, 1958, thirty-two tons (28.6 m tons) of dynamite were detonated, life for 6,500 people was changed forever. The coffer-dams which held the water back over the Long Sault rapids, over the last few months, gave way. The floodwaters of the mighty St. Lawrence River became Lake St. Lawrence, 35 miles (56 km) long and 3.5 miles (5 km) wide, between Cornwall and Iroquois. The water inundated the villages, the farmlands, the road beds, a large section of the land of the early United Empire Loyalists and of their descendants, and indeed, flooded everything left in its passage until July 4th.

It was with feelings of trepidation, sadness, anxiety, and apprehension for some, anger and fear for others, that crowds gathered along the St. Lawrence riverside banks to see the water flooding the shore. A number of sightseeing areas had been set up to allow area residents as well as visitors to witness the rising waters of the mighty St. Lawrence River. Some residents brought their lawn chairs and sat near the river to get a better view of this historic moment. Some gathered with family and friends and stood silently, if not solemnly, in front of the new waters of the St. Lawrence River. Some residents preferred to stay home. It is reported that some residents who feared that the waters would rise too rapidly had moved temporarily away from the area.

People did not know quite what to expect. Some feared that the waters would rise fast, while others feared that the waters would continue rising above expected levels. Some climbed the dyke, which had been built to hold the water of the head pond near Cornwall, and waited for the big blast when the water would come pouring out behind the last coffer-dam. Many expected that a huge, fast-moving wave would follow the blast but instead, at first, saw a trickle of water followed by a steady flow moving towards the Power dam, to reach, at its peak, the equivalent of a sixteen story building.

In fact, the water rose quite slowly. It continued to rise over four days. The four Inundation Days were given names which would reflect the cooperation between both American and Canadian Governments, and, it was hoped, make a contribution to world peace. They were July 1, Dominion Day, July 2, Ontario Day, July 3, City of Cornwall and United Counties Day, and July 4, Independence Day.

Inundation days crystallized for everyone the magnitude of the project and its impact on their lives. Over the four days, everyone came to realize that the familiar terrain, the home land, the ancestral farm, and the village which had been theirs would be lost. Moreover, the familiar roar of the Long Sault rapids would be silenced.

From then on, we would remember the communities which were erased and partly relocated. They were, from east to west, Maple Grove, Mille Roches, Moulinette, Wales, Dickinson's Landing, Santa Cruz, Woodland, Farran's Point, Aultsville, Morrisburg, and Iroquois. We would refer to them as the Lost Villages of the St. Lawrence Seaway and Power project.

The history of those pioneers, the unique architecture of their homes, and their contribution to the riverside communities, survive in our memories.

The Robertson Home

Jeremiah French built his home, in 1784, near the rapids at Mille Roches, in the small hamlet of Maple Grove. As the Seaway project started with the diversion of the County Road #2 between Cornwall and Moulinette, the Maple Grove community was the first one to be displaced. While the small village was relocated, its cemetery was moved in its entirety a few miles west of Cornwall along the new highway.

The French-Robertson home, started by Jeremiah French, and later expanded by his son-in-law, George Robertson, was often referred to as the Maple Grove, its location name. Jeremiah was born in Stratford, Connecticut, on July 8, 1743, son of Loyalist Jeremiah Sr., a land-owning family from Manchester, Vermont. In 1762, Jeremiah married Elizabeth Wheeler and they had six children. He became the town clerk of Manchester, in 1768, and a town constable, in 1774. At the beginning of the American Revolution, Jeremiah joined the British military, as a captain in the 4th Company of the Queen's Loyal Rangers, and later served as a lieutenant of the second battalion of Sir John Johnson's King's Royal Regiment of New York. In the fall of 1778, his farm in Manchester, which had been confiscated, was given to Jared Munson of Massachusetts, and Gideon Ormsby, to be passed on later to Governor Chittenden.

At the end of his military service, on November 24th, 1783, Lieutenant French, a refugee in Canada with his family, received a land grant in the front Seigneurie No. 2 (later re-named Cornwall) of 700 acres and settled along the St. Lawrence River with his young family. Thus, Maple Grove became associated with the Robertson home.

By 1784, French had cleared the land and, contrary to the custom of building a log cabin as a first home, Jeremiah built a timber-frame home measuring sixteen feet by twenty feet (4.9 m by 6.1 m). A kitchen, a bedroom, and a parlour were also added. The frame structure was "insulated" with "salmon" bricks, a form of poorly cured bricks often used at the time. This section of the home survives today as the dining room portion of the Robertson home.

From 1791 to 1796, Jeremiah served in the first Parliament of Upper Canada representing Stormont County, which, at the time, included the townships of Cornwall and Osnabruck extending north to the Ottawa river into the wilderness section of the new colony.

In 1812, Jeremiah sold his property to George Roberston Sr. a prosperous mill owner who had married French's daughter, Elizabeth. At the end of George's service in the war of 1812, he expanded the family home to double its size and included a large parlour and two bedrooms. George renovated the home, added the drawing room at the left side of the home and gave it its neo-classic characteristics: gracious, elegant and orderly facade inspired by the classic Roman and Hellenic styles, the double swag, and pendants of husk moulding. Those features are still preserved today.

Up to the beginning of the Seaway project, the home had been continually occupied by the descendants of the original owners. Thanks to the St. Lawrence Parks Commission, this truly unique home was moved, in 1957, from Maple Grove to the Upper Canada Village Museum and preserved as a legacy given by the descendants of the French and Robertson families. At that time, the dwelling was named the French-Robertson home, in reference to the Village's original objective of representing an early Loyalist village. Recently, the village's orientation has changed to portray an 1860s community of pioneers.

Thus, the Robertson home has been restored to its 19th century appearance, and is presented as the home of the widowed and aged George Robertson, just before his death in 1866.

The Kezar Home

Built by Alvin Kezar in Osnabruck Township on Concession 1, Lot 7, the home was situated in the lost village of Mille Roches. The name Mille Roches is a testimony of the French presence prior to the arrival of the United Empire Loyalists in 1784. Possibly named after its limestone quarry, north of the village, Mille Roches was the land of a 'Thousand Rocks'. It is reported that in 1713, the Governor of New France requested permission from the authorities in France to quarry what was believed to be marble. The limestone quarry was used to provide the raw material necessary to build a number of sections of the Cornwall Canal. Its proximity to the Long Sault rapids may also be another reason for the name Mille Roches. Its true origin has been lost over the years.

Alvin Kezar, born circa 1807, of German descent, was a prosperous merchant living beside the Cornwall Canal and, in the 1851 census, was reported to be a merchant and store keeper. His first wife, Polly, died in 1846. They had two children, Henry and Asaph, born circa 1833 and 1835, respectively. He later married Ellen Martin, of Scottish descent and daughter of James and Jane Martin. Between the years of 1846 to 1850, he sectioned off and sold parts of his lot. Ellen Martin-Kezar passed away on May 1, 1860. As the cemeteries were relocated during the Seaway construction, the Alvin Kezar burial stone was moved to the East Wing, north hall of the Memorial Pioneer Cemetery located on the Upper Canada Village Museum grounds.

The home was later owned by Gregor Bennett, a partner in the Bennett-Messecar medical supplies and pill factory in Mille Roches. The home, situated beside the canal in Mille Roches, was a well known feature in the community. Its four chimneys and beautiful brick exterior made it a very stately home along old Highway #2. It had a high-ceilinged living room with a solid marble fireplace. It is reported that the beauty of the fireplace stone was enhanced by large windows which allowed the sun to shine through.

Verandas were very popular in Upper Canada from 1830 to 1855. They were often built across the front and sides of the home, sometimes extending to the kitchen wings at the rear. The Regency Ontario Cottage of the mid 1800s often saw the appearance of posts and brackets later replaced by elaborate treillage, or decorative trellis.

The Kezar home had some decorative brackets on wooden posts with diamond-shaped treillage which supported the veranda roof, and a hipped roof culminating in a square cupola. The home had an elaborate front door with elliptical shaped transom and side lights. It is a fine example of the square-plan type of home with its wrap-around veranda on three sides of the two-storey home. The home shows features of the Regency as well as the Revival Italianate styles - the tall rectangular round-headed windows added to the cupola, and the elaborate type of home.

For a number of years leading up to the Seaway project, Lera Fyckes lived in the home. It is with fondness that she is remembered singing along with the choir while playing the "pump organ" in the United Church, a few doors west of the home.

Although the home was destroyed in 1954 to allow for the construction of the Seaway project, the fireplace was preserved in the house built for Lera Fyckes in Long Sault.

The McNairn Home

The Loyalists had a strong influence on the domestic architecture of Upper Canada. The first dwelling which followed the log home was the one or two-storey square or rectangular home referred to as the Georgian or the Loyalist home followed by the Regency style home.

The McNairn home is a fine example of the side-hall plan home which the Loyalists introduced later. The side-hall plan resulted when the front door of the square home was moved under the gable end. A side wing was further added to produce an "ell" shape dwelling, popularized in the 1840s. Roof lines varied from low to high pitch with gable ends. Stoops, verandas, and porches with wooden posts or elaborate treillage decorated the exterior of the homes.

The McNairn home was located along the St. Lawrence River in the strip village of Mille Roches with its back facing the Cornwall Canal approximately four miles (6.4 km) west of Cornwall on Highway #2. The greater part of the village of Mille Roches was situated on land originally granted to Abraham Marsh, a United Empire Loyalist who settled on Lots 25 and 26 in the first concession of the town of Cornwall. It is said that his daughter, Sarah Marsh, married Adam Dixson of Moulinette.

Some of the Empire Loyalists who received land grants in the area were the Brownell, the Summer, the Milross, the Annable, the Sheets, the Raymond, the Tait, the Tilton, the Brook, and the McNairn families. The early Loyalists settled on the shores at Mille Roches nearest to the river severed from the mainland by the Cornwall canal. This area became known as "Old Mille Roches" . A swing bridge connected "Old Mille Roches" to the mainland.

John Mc Nairn, who had fought in the King's Regiment and had lost all personal property, belonged to the Bateau Company of the Regiment, under the command of Captain Josh Herchimer. Prior to the war of 1783, there were very few settlements west of Montreal because travel was very difficult due to numerous rapids along the river. However, during and after the war, troops and refugees who moved west needed the river to transport goods and provisions. The Bateau Regiment ensured that the flat-bottom freight boats fought their way successfully up the river all the way to Fort Erie and beyond.

In the late spring of 1784, John McNairn received one hundred acres of land in the area of Cornwall (formerly known as Seigneurie No. 2 and New Johnston), near Barnhart Island. Family genealogical records show that John McNairn was a Sergeant in the Kings Royal Regiment of New York while his son, Alexander McNairn, was a Lieutenant in the 2nd Regiment of Stormont. Alexander would have been twenty years old during the war of 1812-1814.

Furthermore, it is said that John McNairn made a claim for compensation for losses suffered. His claim said that he was a native of Scotland and came to Canada in 1778. He also claimed to have been taken prisoner twice, to have developed a farm on the Susquehanna, and to have cleared fifteen acres of land. For his losses, he received a compensation of sixty pounds sterling - a substantial amount for the times.

The McNairn farm would have celebrated its centennial year in 1958 had it not been for the St. Lawrence project which cut short its life. Displeased with the Ontario Hydro assessment value for their home, the McNairns presented their case to the Ontario Municipal Board and were granted additional compensation which served mostly to cover legal fees.

Stanley McNairn, descendant of John McNairn, and a local journalist historian decided to moved his home along County Road #2 near Cornwall in Lakeview Heights. This area was created to receive a number of homes previously situated between the various villages. With the original roof and bricks, he rebuilt the exterior of the home, adding a closed-in porch to replace the ancestral front veranda.

Considering the turmoil caused by the move, Mrs. McNairn, who was expecting a child, returned to Ireland for the birth of her son.

On August 23, 2003, the McNairn family held a reunion and shared fond memories of life in the old village.

The Messecar Home

Dr. Messecar's home was built in 1904, facing the river in the west end of Mille Roches. The village of Mille Roches had a slow early development. In 1856, the Grand Trunk Railway brought some growth to the small village. However, at the turn of the century, with the building of the dam at Sheek's Island, and the enlargement of the Cornwall Canal, the village experienced renewed prosperity. There were the Guy Cutler's carriage works, the Lewis Derocher's inn, the Israel Brook's chairmaking shop, the Simon Ault's carding mills, the Whitcomb Kezar's general store, one tailor shop, and some mills.

With the possibility of generating power, Mille Roches was able to expand. From the development of its sawmills and its limestone quarry to its successful furniture business fifty years earlier, the village welcomed the arrival, in 1904, of the Cornwall Paper Manufacturing Company. Although the paper mill changed hands a number of times, it provided permanency to the village and allowed it to grow to more than eight hundred. There were five stores, a large arena, two service stations, two restaurants, a school and three churches.

Dr. John Messecar was born in 1870 at Waterford, Ontario. Prior to his graduation from the University of Toronto in 1898 with an MB (Bachelor of Medicine) degree, John Messecar attended Port Dover High School. Shortly after his graduation, he moved to Mille Roches and established his medical practice which would last well into the 1940s.

As a dedicated country doctor, he would do what was necessary to keep his community healthy. Delivering babies, pulling teeth and fitting dentures were some tasks required of a country doctor. Assisted by his equally dedicated nurse, Janet McLellan-Welch, he traveled on dirt roads, country roads, and ice-bridges in the winter to provide the best care for his patients in remote areas. It is reported that his nurse would always keep a few freshly starched uniforms for those rounds which would last three or four days due to weather or road conditions. As

times were difficult for many families, and in the absence of medicare, the doctor and the nurse would often return home with items such as a bag of potatoes.

In addition to his faithful service to his patients, Dr. Messecar would ensure that, day or night, he was able to carry on his house calls. He would tend to his horse, continually overseeing to its good health as well as the road worthiness of his buggy. Both were essential for his rounds. By association, Dr. Messecar exemplifies the commitment and dedication of all country doctors.

He lived in the home until his death in 1944. His wife, Mary Elise Ryerson, continued to occupy it until Louise, their daughter, married and started her family in the Messecar home. The white home with red rustic trim had a large front porch above which was a canopied balcony. A side door with a matching porch would welcome patients of Dr. Messecar. In 1935, the front porch was closed in. The extended family lived in the home until 1956 when it was sold to Ontario Hydro and was moved to Long Sault during the Seaway project.

It is now the home of the Long Sault Legion. The Longue (sic) Sault Royal Canadian Legion branch which had served the communities of Mille Roches and Moulinette since April 2nd. 1946 gave up its Charter and moved to Long Sault.

On November 21st, 1957, a new Charter was issued by the Canadian Legion of the British Empire Service League. Under the branch number 569, the new Long Sault Legion has continued to serve its community out of the Messecar home.

The McLellan Home

The McLellan home was built by Angus McLellan, circa 1885, on an eight acre property in Mille Roches. Inspired by the Second Empire Revival building style originated after Confederation, between 1860 to 1890 years, the home's most important distinguishing feature is its gambrel roof. Although many of the homes with the double pitch roof tended to be square in design, some adopted the "L" (or ell) shape such as the McLellan's.

The McLellan home, which was moved from Mille Roches to Long Sault, was inherited by Alexander McLellan, nephew of Angus McLellan. When the first World War erupted in 1914, Alexander Joseph and Archibald Eugene McLellan, brothers born at Mille Roches, and sons of Isabel Ann (Bella) McDonell and Alexander Eugene McLellan, enlisted and served in the Canadian Expeditionary Force. Their two other brothers, Aeneas Benedict and James Edmund born in Quebec, also enlisted and served in the same force.

Alexander Joseph, the oldest of the family, was born in 1890. Wounded by shrapnel in 1917, Alex had his left arm amputated. Following the war, he settled in Mille Roches on the property inherited from his uncle, Angus. He resumed operation of the honey and beekeepers business, which had been managed by his two sisters, Mary and Janet, during his absence. Alex also served as the local postmaster for a number of years.

Aeneas (Mac) Benedict was born on December 6, 1893 in Coteau, Quebec, while his father was engaged in the boat-building industry in Valleyfield. Mac was only nine years old at the time of his mother's death in 1902. In 1916, Mac enlisted in the Royal Canadian Engineers, and went overseas. He was discharged at the end of the war with a right shoulder injury caused by shrapnel. He died in Cornwall in 1970 at the age of 77.

The other two sons were killed in action. Archibald (Archie) Eugene was killed on November 18, 1916 at the age of 19. While Archie has no known grave, his name is commemorated on the Vimy Memorial, France, in the Book of Remembrance, Parliament Buildings, Ottawa, on the War Memorial formerly in Mille Roches and moved to Long Sault, and in the Commonwealth War Games Commission Internet Website. Young James, of D Company, was hit, while he was responsible for moving ammunition up the front, during an attack on the enemy's position. James (Jim) Edmund, the youngest in the family, was killed on August 8, 1918 at the age of 19.

In 1916, Janet and Mary, sisters of the above brothers, graduated from Hotel Dieu Hospital Nursing program, in Kingston. After a short nursing service in Montreal, Janet returned to Mille Roches and, in 1917, she married Lawrence Welch at our Lady of Grace Church (destroyed during the Seaway), in Dickinson's Landing. When she became widowed in 1936, she returned to her career and worked in close collaboration with Dr. Messecar, also from Mille Roches.

During the Seaway construction, Hydro Ontario purchased the McLellan home from Oscar Eamon, who had bought it from Alex MacGillivray, and moved it to Long Sault, next door to the Messecar home. Mary, on the other hand married Bruce Vandervort and spent the rest of her life in Michigan and in Florida.

The McLellan boys, who fought so bravely in World War I for their country, were followed by nephews Donald, Lawrence and Edward (sons of Janet McLellan-Welch) from Mille Roches in the second World War. In 1946, along with their one hundred comrades from Mille Roches, which at the time had a population of approximately seven hundred, they were honored at a banquet held to recognize their contribution to Canadian life.

The memorial moved to Long Sault in memory of those who died reads: *1914-1918 In grateful and undying memory of those who gave their all Laurence Edgar Abbott, Charles Sydney Antoine, Allan Hickey, George Lunn, Frederick Lama, Archibald Eugene McLellan, James Edmund McLellan, Arthur Runions, William Milross Roys. RESURGANT.*

The Johnston Home

With the Seaway and Power Project signed agreement between Canada and the United States on May 13, 1953, employment in the community became very unstable. The Provincial Paper Mill, which was the major area employer at the time, closed its doors and moved its equipment to Thorold, Ontario. Some families left to follow employment. Some stayed and faced the disappearance of their old village.

By August 1954, the construction of the Seaway project was underway. While a number of homes were left behind, only two brick homes from Mille Roches were moved to Long Sault, the new village created to receive the displaced residents. They were the Hugh Warner home and the Ezra Johnston home, both moved to Mille Roches Road, in Long Sault.

The Johnston centennial home was built by Ezra Allan Johnston for his family in Mille Roches. Ezra, who cut the lumber himself, began construction in 1904, and completed the home in 1908. Mr. Johnston solicited the help of Leslie Manson, who owned a store in Mille Roches, George Desrosiers, and Herbert Brooks for the construction of his new home. In fact, the period of construction corresponds exactly to the four years of the Seaway construction period. In 2004, the Johnston home will celebrate its one hundredth year, thus its appellation centennial home.

Fifty years later, in 1957, the James William Hartshorne House Moving Company relocated this thirty-two ton (29 m tons) home to Long Sault for Ontario Hydro.

Over the years, the home had been passed on to the children in the family. By the arrival of the Seaway project, a number of families had lived there, including the O'Neil family. At the end of the construction, Mr. O'Neil, an engineer, who had been employed by the Angus McDonald Construction Company of Cornwall to work on the project, returned to Ireland with his family. The home was left empty and was then repossessed by Ontario Hydro which held the mortgage.

In 1965, the home was sold to the present owners who have enjoyed it ever since. The nine children, who have grown up in the Long Sault home, have fond memories of their centennial home.

The Johnston home shares its style between the Georgian and Italianate influences. Its two stories, good proportions, even number of shuttered bays on each side of the front entrance and its low hipped roof are features of the Georgian-Loyalist home. Its squareness of form and projecting veranda are reminders of the large Italian villas, although much less elaborate. The original embossed gilded tin ceilings, stained glass window transoms, and beveled glass in the front door have been preserved with great care. Over the years the old kitchen made room for new oak door cupboards, and a sun room was added at the rear.

Suffering from serious wood rot, a new front veranda was built recently almost duplicating its original form. The walls in the living and dining room are re-waxed twice a year and the century home continues to sparkle with life again.

The present owners, who have appreciated the history of their home, have continually attempted to maintain its beauty and its historical integrity.

The Raymond Home

Sheek's island, approximately two miles (3.20 km) long and three-quarters of a mile (1.2 km)wide, was situated in the most attractive part of the St. Lawrence River, i.e. east of the mighty Long Sault Rapids, west of Cornwall, and south of the villages Moulinette and Mille Roches.

The well-wooded island, which was partially flooded in 1958, was also a land rich in native history. Indeed, Sheek's island was Indian territory. At the beginning of the construction of the Seaway project, it was the site of archeological digs under the supervision of Dr. J. Norman Emerson, Supervisor of Archeological Studies at the University of Toronto's Department of Anthropology, during the summers of 1956 and 1957. Old and young dug to find treasures. Archeologists, engineers, teachers, students, and librarians came to search for artifacts before the island was flooded. A good number of artifacts belonging to Point Peninsular Indians have been found dating as far back as 3,500 years.

In addition to its treasures and to a magnificent view of the Long Sault Rapids, Sheek's island was the site of the Ault Park which was situated at the head, or west end, of Sheek's island facing the Long Sault Rapids. This well-wooded area offered an exceptional view of the St. Lawrence River and of the Long Sault rapids. It was an ideal place for picnics, swimming, and family gatherings.

The park was named upon a request of Levis (Lewis) Addison Ault of Cincinnati, Ohio, who, in 1914, had purchased forty acres of land at the west end of the island to be reserved as parkland and, as a memorial to his mother and father, presented it to his township. Mr. Levis (Lewis) Addison Ault was born in Moulinette in 1851. He was the great grandson of John Ault, grandson of Nicholas John Ault, and son of Simon William Ault and his wife Caroline Brownell, of United Empire Loyalist descent. Mr. Ault, whose ancestors fought in the American War of Independence and who is a descendant of the Aults of Osnabruck and Cornwall Township, died in 1930.

Sheek's Island was named after David Sheek who had settled there at the beginning of the nineteenth century. Considering the ideal farming conditions, there were a few families who lived on the island year round and farmed its approximately fourteen hundred acres. There were also a few cottages along its west end. Over the years since 1800, the island had been linked to the mainland by a timber bridge and a tunnel. There was also a swing bridge and a tunnel connecting the island with Mille Roches. However, with the construction of the canals in the mid-1800's, the tunnels were flooded.

In 1955, as the bridge could not be used to transport buildings saved from the flood, the fate of the homes and cottages on the island was sealed. Thus, in an effort to save some one hundred island cottages, Island 17, Island 18, and Ault Island were reserved for cottage owners. The summer homes were slid over the ice to their new sites during the winters of 1956 and 1957. All other homes were destroyed by fire or demolition.

Another one of the original families who lived on the island was the Raymond family whose ancestors had come from the Mohawk Valley during the Loyalist immigration. A number of other Raymond family members cultivated the island up to 1954.

The solid stone structure, home of Wilfred and Ruby Raymond, like all other homes, was destroyed to make way for the flood waters.

The Dixson Home

Around 1820, Adam Dixson (also spelled Dixon) built this two-storey neo-Georgian or Loyalist neo-classic brick house referred to as the Miller's house. It was a majestic home with side wings, facing the canal, along the St. Lawrence River. The left wing housed a study and an office while a kitchen and a pantry were situated in the right wing. His home, on the banks of the river at Moulinette, housed his family of three children.

The Dixson home demonstrates a good example of a unique feature of Eastern Ontario homes. When covered front porch roofs needed replacing, the owner would often choose not to repair, causing the second storey door to be known as the suicide door.

Adam ran a general store in Moulinette, developed the towpath (riverside path created to enable upriver going batteaux to be pulled by horses or cattle), became Moulinette Postmaster, and developed the real estate in the area. He provided much support for the early development of Moulinette and was one of the contractors for the Cornwall canal completed in 1842. Adam Dixson obtained a license for Innkeeping in about 1801 and kept it until it lapsed in 1825.

Adam was the son of John Dixson, a United Empire Loyalist who owned eleven acres of land in the Albany County of New York when the American War of Independence erupted. When John joined the King's Loyal Americans, also known as the King's Loyal Ranger or Jessup's Corps, he left behind all personal possessions.

In a sworn statement signed by John Dixson, and dated April 1775, he claimed his losses to be at two hundred and thirty pounds, one shilling and nine pence, New York currency. Included in his statement is a list of items he lost, such as two "house dwellings", a stable, six acres of planted potatoes and corn, household furniture, bed "cloaths", farming essentials, carpenters tools, fifteen bushels of Indian corn, and four cows. His petition for compensation includes the reason which he writes " between the 15th July 1783 and the 25th March 1784 resided in the District of Montreal and was doing duty as a soldier till the 24th December 1783 which prevented the delivery of this claim."

At the end of the war, he applied for land in the Old Lunenburg District. Together with his wife, Elizabeth, daughter of Sir John Johnson, and his three young children, he settled on a land grant of 200 acres situated on the entire west half of Lot 31 in the first concession, and the east half of Lot 32. Over the next few years, he also acquired Lot 17, in the second concession of Cornwall Township, and the west half of Lot 32 in the second concession of the same Township. Thus, it is said that the Dixsons were the first family to settle in Moulinette.

John Dixson and his son, Adam, became prominent businessmen of the Eastern District of Upper Canada as early as 1803. John Dixson acquired a sawmill known as Dixson's Mill, woollen, and grist mills which were operated by hydro power produced by a dam which he built between Sheek's Island and Moulinette. He also erected two locks for which he charged a toll, to the disapproval of the government of the times. In 1808, John Dixson sold his land and his family business to his son, Adam, who pursued his father's interests.

In addition to his success as a businessman, Adam was a prominent member of the Reform party and served in the Second Regiment of the Stormont Militia. It is said that, as a Justice of Peace, he brought fairness to the canal workers. Moreover, he was instrumental in the development of Trinity Episcopal Church in Cornwall, and, in 1834, made funds and land available for the construction of Christ Church in Moulinette.

Today, Christ Church stands at the Upper Canada Village Museum in memory of Adam Dixson who died on May 9, 1837. His funeral was held in the church before its actual completion that year.

Adam was buried in the graveyard of the Christ Church of which he was a founder.

The Dixson Home and Front Door

The death of Adam Dixson, in the spring of 1837, brought about the beginning of the decline of the family business and of the village of Moulinette. However, with the access to transport provided by the Grand Trunk railway, in 1854, the strip village experienced new growth. It had one general store, two churches (Anglican Christ Church, now at Upper Canada Village and the destroyed Methodist Church), two hotels (The Lion and the Pea Green), a barber shop (Zina Hill Barber Shop, now at the Lost Villages Museum), a garage, and a century-old school house.

It is not known if the Dixson home, on the banks of the river at Moulinette, originally housed John's family. The salmon-buff brick home, of neo-classic style, was built by his son, Adam Dixson, circa 1820. In the 1861 census, it was reported that the house was owned by George Dixson, grand-son of John Dixson, and son of Adam Dixson and Sarah Marsh. George is described as a 40-year old man, born in Upper Canada, Church of England, single, and residing in a two-storey brick house with a male member of the family.

The grand old mansion was born when people were looking for large and roomy homes. Since the Dixsons were Loyalists from Virginia, they were familiar with the plantation mansions of the south. Bringing their customs and culture with them, the Dixsons built their home to reflect those grand styles. It was known for its tall arched doorways and its ceiling railings which were reminiscent of a royal crown. The Dixson home had six fireplaces, including twin mantels in the ballroom situated in the centre of the home on the second floor.

Although at the time of the Seaway the home was still in the hands of the Dixson descendants, it had been left vacant for a number of years. In 1954, it was indeed difficult to recognize its original beauty including the wings which, originally, were parallel to the main portion of the house but had been demolished over the years. Although these side wings were gone they were clearly traceable. The decorative roof balustrade and the large veranda were also gone. The dining room door still had traces of undyed mahogany. The two colored-glass panels of the arched front doorways, on each floor, created a dramatic entrance to the elegant home. However, the front door, as well as its other interior wood trims, had suffered damage during years of neglect.

During the Seaway construction, plans were made to save and preserve the old neglected home by moving it to the Upper Canada Village Museum. After a number of plans were drawn and blue prints were prepared to restore the home, it was estimated too costly to bring the old structure back to life. Therefore, the home was demolished. Some internal fittings and wood trim went for conservation to the Royal Ontario Museum in Toronto.

The Dixson home is a testimony of the vision and leadership demonstrated by those ancestors who built early communities.

The Johnston Home

The Johnston home, at one time the property of Annie Dixson, a relative of Sir John Johnson, was moved from the center of the village of Moulinette to the new County Road #2 by the Sullivan Moving Company. From 1948 to the mid-1960's, Wendell and Melba Johnston and their five children lived in the home.

The Johnston home's rather familiar exterior belies its unique interior. Historically, as a home owner's financial situation improved, so did his home. The Johnston home was built in two time periods. The right side of the home is more than 200 years old while the left side of the home was added before the turn of the twentieth century. Features of the original home such as wide beams, thick walls, and narrow encased stairway still can be seen today.

While restoring the hearth on the original section of the home, the present owners found an 1825 newspaper amongst the many layers of brick, stone, and mortar. Amongst the unique features of the newer section of the home (on the left side) which have been preserved, we can still appreciate the original fireplace and a wide entrance hallway divided from the dining room with a pair of glass sliding doors above which is a semi-elliptical fanlight transom. Aside from a few recent renovations, including a front veranda, the home has maintained much of its unique features which the various owners have appreciated over the years.

The relocation required an equivalent compensation of three acres of land which the family had obtained under the veterans land act and, which the new village of Long Sault could not accommodate. The home was, therefore, moved east of Long Sault. During the move across the railroad track, the flat bed tires blew and the train between Moulinette and Mille Roches was cancelled for one day.

Prior to the Seaway project, the village of Moulinette, west of Mille Roches, spread along the St. Lawrence River slightly less than one mile (1.6 km) on either side of Highway #2. Although the home was situated north of the highway, children in the family remember the enjoyment provided by their surroundings and the easy access to the river for swimming, fishing, and boating.

The village was settled on land granted to Sir John Johnson at the end of the war. Sir John Johnson, who was born in America in 1742, moved through the ranks of Cadet in the New York Provincials to Captain to Major General, in 1776. In 1780, he was appointed Lieutenant-Colonel of the King's Royal Regiment of New York. By 1784, when he became land owner of lots in Montreal, Cataraqui (Kingston), and the Royal Township #1 (Cornwall), he was married to Mary (Polly) Watts, and had five children. On May 1784, as Superintendent-General, he was assigned the responsibility of the refugee Loyalists re-settlement.

Records show that the origin of the name Moulinette is unclear. It may mean the translation of winch, or wheels, which the french merchants and fur traders of the 18th century used to pull their batteaux up stream. It may also be reminiscent of the numerous mills along the river, as well as the water mills created by the rapids.

Another early settler of Moulinette was John Gray Goodall Snetsinger who owned a saw and a grist mills, and operated a general store where he traded goods from Montreal with butter, grain, and wood from local farmers. Steamboats made scheduled stops at Mr. Snetsinger's wharf, for the exchange of cargoes. Area farmers found additional income by supplying the steamboats with cordwood. Mr. Snetsinger served as a member of Parliament for Stormont from 1896 to 1900. Through his efforts, in 1910, a small train station, used as a waiting room, was erected for the village. The small station now stands at the Lost Villages Museum along the relocated County Road #2 in Ault Park, east of Long Sault.

The story is told by the present owners that the Sullivan Moving Company also moved a number of homes during the construction of the Seaway and Power project. In fact, while moving a home to its new site one day, an unexpected strong wind blew and tipped it into the ditch. After a quick assessment, the company decided to set it ablaze and compensate the owners.

The Johnston Home and the "Inside Inn"

The Johnston home, also known as the "Inside Inn", was owned by Mabel and Harry Johnston. The home was originally located in the middle of the village of Moulinette and backed onto the St. Lawrence River.

The St. Lawrence River was a very attractive stretch of waterfront for residents and tourists. In stage-coach times, the old Johnston home served as a staging house and inn and was known for years as The Pea Green Hotel. From the 1930's it was owned by the Johnston family. All six of the Johnston children grew up at the Inside Inn. Naturally, swimming, boating, and fishing were most popular with the family. Mr. and Mrs. Johnston delighted in their large and varied vegetable garden as well as their wide assortment of flowers and shrubs. Their home was a frequent destination point for relatives and friends.

The Inn burned to the ground in September 1949. It happened during a night when all members of the family were away for the weekend. The day following the fire, while Mr. Johnston was sadly scanning the ruins, he was heard to remark, "I guess we can build a new home on this foundation!" And so Mr. and Mrs. Johnston arranged to have a new home built on the old foundation once the charred remains were cleared away. The new home was occupied during the winter of 1949-1950. It continued to be used as the Inside Inn. The plans for the new home had included a sunroom overlooking the river.

During the early 1950's, when the Ontario Hydro home-purchasing crews were circulating in the old villages, Mrs. Johnston was fighting cancer and never got to see the development of the town of Long Sault, or the completion of the Seaway. Mr. Johnston sold the home to Hydro Ontario and built a new, smaller one in Long Sault. The "Old Inside Inn" was then moved to Long Sault on Bethune Street. It is a cement block home which was moved in 1957.

The village of Moulinette was situated north of Sheek's island and Bergin Lake created during the continuous improvements made to the original canals. In 1870, a dam was built between Sheek Island and the north shores, about two miles west of Moulinette. Although there was a culvert under the canal, a bridge also joined the island from the mainland. At Mille Roches to the east, a dam and electrical power generating station were also built.

These dams resulted in the creation of a lake three miles (4.8 km) long and one-half mile (.8 km) wide, named Bergin Lake in honor of Dr. Danby Bergin who was born in Toronto, attended Upper Canada College, and later Mc Gill University, in Montreal. Prior to his death on October 22, 1896, Dr. Bergin had served as Colonel of the old 59th Stormont and Glengarry Battalion.

The early mills which were driven by water-power disappeared under Bergin Lake, while others were built later.

It is with fondness that family and friends remember the beauty of the landscape and the spell of the river on visitors. Indeed, the meandering road along the canals, by the islands, along the Long Sault Rapids, and through the villages shaded by the old trees, attracted tourists of all kinds - the fishermen, the boaters, the cottagers, the trappers, and the holidayers.

The present owners, Barbara and Ray Fenton, who bought the home from Margarie and Clifford Stevenson, have been in the house for thirty-two years and continue to enjoy its unique history.

The Dafoe Home

Close proximity of the Canadian and American shores along the St. Lawrence River favoured the development of friendly ties amongst the riverside communities ever since the days of the first explorers. Trading, as well as social partnerships, had evolved over the years. Canadians and Americans hunted together, fished together, and married within each other's families.

Barnhart Island was barely half a mile (.8 km)from Maple Grove. It was approximately two miles wide (3.2 km) and covered over seventeen hundred acres of land. The island, Canadian land until the war of 1812 -1814, was situated south of Sheek's island. The magnificent Long Sault rapids flowed eastward, at its north-west end. The island was the size of a small hamlet with its two roads, a few mills, a school, and a church. In 1950, the last island resident, Edgar Mullarney, moved to Massena when the island was taken over and became the American side of the Moses-Saunders Power Dam.

It is said that the island was named after William George Barnhart who had come from Holland or Germany and had settled in the state of New York, on the banks of the Delaware, prior to the War of Independence. As a United Empire Loyalist, and entitled to a land grant, George petitioned King George III for the island. In 1796, he was granted permission to lease the land from the Mohawk Indians, at St. Regis, and in 1804, there he settled.

In 1814, the island became the object of a settlement, through the Treaty of Ghent, which gave the island back to the United States while Canada, for strategic reasons, retained Wolfe island further west in the St. Lawrence River.

When the Loyalists fled to the north in 1784 they turned their backs on the land they had cultivated for a number of years. They also left behind family ties and the country which had originally welcomed them. It is reported that when the American Civil war erupted in 1861, some Loyalists, living in Upper Canada, either volunteered to fight for the north or were paid by Americans to stand in as soldiers for them. Indeed, some descendants of a number of Loyalist Canadian veterans, who had moved to Canada after the war of 1784, returned to fight for the North in the American Civil War.

Other veterans, of American origin, married and settled in Upper Canada only to return to their land of birth to defend it. It is reported that Alexander and George Carbino, twin brothers, were born on Barnhart's Island, in 1843, of Mary Fromboys and Charles Carbino. The 1851 Census for the Cornwall Township, in Stormont county, lists six Carbino family members. However, their name is spelled Carbino and Carbineau, as it is also spelled in French.

George settled in Massena, New York, while Alexander moved to the Township of Osnabruck, Canada. At the age of forty, Alexander married (second marriage) Hanna Hesson, age twenty, from Osnabruck Township. Alexander and Hanna died in December 1943, and July 1955, respectively. Alexander and Hanna had five children, one of whom was Elwood Carbino who was born on December 27, 1903, and died on September 10, 1994.

Five brothers of the Charles Carbino family enlisted in the American Civil War. Alexander, who had enlisted as a private in the cavalry under Captain Julius Windebeck, and served in a number of battles, was enrolled on July 10th 1863, to serve three years. Family records show that T. L. Lee, first Lieutenant, signed his discharge on September 21, 1865 at the end of the war.

The descendants of Alexander Carbino's family presently live in the restored and expanded Carl Dafoe family home. In 1954, the Carl Dafoe family owned the ell shape clapboard home built circa 1900.

The home moved from Farran's Point to Ingleside, continues to be a proud reminder of our close relationship with our neighbors to the south.

The Hoople Home

Hoople's Creek used to meander along the western side of the lost village of Wales before the Seaway construction. Aside from the numerous pleasures the creek gave to the children in the form of nature exploration and fishing, the creek was a watershed area for the land north of the St. Lawrence River. Its fame is preserved by two important events which carved its place in history: the American militia attack in the battle of 1812 and the famous "Granny Hoople", medicine woman.

In addition to being named after Colonel Hoople who held back the American militia at the battle of Crysler's farm, the small creek claimed its place in history because of the woman who became an historical figure in the area. Affectionately known as Granny Hoople, Mary Whitmore, as the first medicine woman, was a legend in her time. At a young age, her family home in Pennsylvania had been raided by native Indians and revolutionaries. During her years of captivity within an Indian family, she learned the art of herbal medicine, the resources provided by the forest, and developed the gift of healing.

Later, Mary returned to her family and was re-united with her uncle Jacob Sheets. She met, in 1788, and married Henry Hoople. Henry and his brother, John, United Empire Loyalist descendants, were some of the first few settlers to arrive and build their homes on the shores of the St. Lawrence River. Henry and John, who had fought in Sir Johnson's colonial troops, the King's Royal Regiment of New York, settled on Lot 11 of the first concession of Osnabruck township.

In 1805, Henry and Mary built a new home, which was to be one of six homes they would build in the area of the second concession of Osnabruck township. Indeed, records show that in 1804, Andrew Gibson, who had been granted one hundred acres of land sold the entire lot to Henry Hoople, who, in turn, sold it to his brother, John, in 1826. The lot was sold for five shillings, Halifax currency. Witnesses to the transaction were John Weart, Nelson Hoople (a relative of the Hoople brothers) and Thomas Moss.

The Illustrated Historical Atlas of the counties records the marriage of John Hoople and Eleanor Kintnor as the first marriage celebrated in the Township of Osnabruck. The ceremony is reported to have been held under the boughs of an old oak tree, close to the river on Lot 11.

Local history reports, that in 1812, an attack took place on the Canadian shore by the American General Wilkinson, on his way to the government stores in Cornwall, a preliminary step before the taking of Montreal. The skirmish left an American soldier wounded near the home of Colonel Hoople. Mary and her sister-in-law, Eleanor Kintnor, cared for the dying American soldier. For over sixty years, before local physicians were available, Mary also used her medicinal skills to care for the sick and dying.

Situated on Manning Road, it is not known which of the six Hoople homes this one would be. However, it is said that this home was one of the first dwellings built on the "Old Post Road". Over the years, it had served as a weigh station as well as a stopover stage coach home. Records show that the original home had a number of dormer windows to enhance lighting in the upper storey. Although the home of Mary Whitmore is not easily recognizable today, more than one hundred seventy years later, descendants of the Hoople family lived in the home at the time of the Seaway Project. Still on its original stone foundation and beams, the home was expanded in 1989.

Today Hoople's Creek is more than a creek. Since the flooding of 1958, it has become a network of small creeks pouring into a large bay separated from the St. Lawrence River by a causeway along County Road #2.

The Stuart Home Before 1954

The history of the lost village of Wales is closely tied to the Stuart family, upon whose land the village was built.

It was originally settled by Dr. James Stuart, who had arrived in America from Scotland with his young family, including five boys, in July 1774 and settled in Delaware. He had purchased one hundred acres of land. It is said that in 1777, amongst precious possessions, he owned four horses, two heifers, two steers, sheep, lab equipment, farming utensils, books, and surgical instruments.

Since Dr. James Stuart had faithfully served in the King's regiment until the end of the War of Independence he was entitled to a land grant. As a surgeon in the British Army of the King's Royal Regiment, in 1785, he had received six hundred acres of land from King George III for his dedicated service.

In 1783, Lord Dorchester, Governor of Quebec from 1766 to 1778, and later again, from 1786 to 1796, became the Commander-in-Chief of the British forces in North America. He was responsible for the evacuation of the faithful Loyalists, thirty thousand troops, and the twenty-seven thousand refugees from the United States.

Also known as Sir Guy Carleton, the Right Honorable Lord Dorchester proclaimed, by Order-in-Council dated November 9th, 1789, the granting of land to those who had defended the British Crown in the war with the United States, in 1784. The document, which is written under the Old British Province of Quebec, grants land in the new Seigneuries established in 1783.

In the presence of thirteen members of the council as well as the Honorable William Smith, Esquire, and Chief Justice, the document was signed by J. Williams, Esquire, confirming the granting of land to the faithful soldiers. It also outlined the conditions to be met in its application.

The text of the law reads:
> "The Council concurring with his Lordship, it is accordingly Ordered:

That the several Land Boards take courfe for the preserving a Regiftry of the names of all Perfons, falling under the description aforementioned, to the End that their Pofterity may be difcriminated, from future Settlers, in the Parifh Regifters and Rolls of the Militia of their respective Districts, and other Public Remembrancers of the Province, as proper Objects, by their preferving of the Fidelyti and Conduct, fo honourable to their Ancestors, for diftinguifhed Benefits and Privileges.

It is alfo Ordered, that the faid Land Boards may, in every fuch Case, provide not only for the Sons of thofe Loyalifts, as they arrive to Full Age, but for their Daughters alfo, of that Age, or on their marriage, affigning to each a Lot of Two Hundred Acres, more of lefs, provided neverthelefs that they refpectively comply with the general Regulations and that it fhall fatifactorily appear, that there has been no Default in the due Cultivation and Improvements of the Lands already affigned to the Head of the Family, of which they are Members.

Built in 1810, the Stuart ancestral home was situated on land owned by Dr. James Stuart in the village of Wales. This view of the back door also shows the lush forest surrounding his farmland. Five generations of the Stuart family lived on his property.

It was facing Stuart Creek which ran into Hoople's Creek before pouring into the St. Lawrence River.

The Stuart Home After 1958

In his Certificate numbered 3882, confirming his grant, under the Old British Province of Quebec, in the Osnabruck Township, Dr. James Stuart's land grant reads:

Province of Quebec, Quebec, 24th November, 1785.

The Bearer hereof, James Stuart, doctor, wife and child - Loyalists being entitled to Six Hundred Acres of Land, by his Majefty's Inftructions to the Governor of this Province, has drawn a Lot (No 7 & 8, in the 1st. and 2nd Concefsion) confifting of Six hundred acres in part of the faid Proportion, in the Seigneurie of Third Township and having taken the Oaths, and made and figned the Declaration required by the Insftructions, he is hereby authorifed to fettle and improve the faid Lot, without delay; and being fettled thereon, he fhall receive a Deed of Conceffion at the expiration of Twelve Months from the Date hereof.

Henry Hamilton

By Order of his Honor, the Lieutenant Governor,

John Collins, LG.

The lost village of Wales was situated inland, north of Dickinson's Landing and north east of Hoople's Creek. The Stuart land stretched from the St. Lawrence River northward to the new County Road #2. As the entire village of Wales, situated almost one mile (1.6 kilometer) inland from the St. Lawrence River, was lower than the two hundred forty-two (73.8 km) feet above sea level required for the new St. Lawrence Lake, it would be flooded by 1958. Therefore, the expansion of the St. Lawrence River required the purchase of four farms in the area - the Morrison's, the Dickson's, the Malone's, and the Stuart's. A good section of the Stuart land was purchased from Wallace and Linda Stuart by Ontario Hydro, in 1955.

As a portion of Stuart land was saved, the family home was moved to the upper section of the Stuart land, north of the new County Road #2. Although the home changed hands a number of times over the years, it remained in the family.

The present owner, who had lived in the home his entire life, passed away recently. He remembered, with fond memories, the cold winter nights and the difficulty experienced by the family to heat the non-insulated home with coal and wood. Temperatures of ten degrees outside translated into thick frost around the windows on the inside. Moreover, he appreciated its long and unique history associated with the United Empire Loyalists of the late 1700's.

The Union Cemetery, directly south of the highway and located on the northern portion of Stuart land, safe from the flood waters, became the new site of all the relocated cemeteries along the St. Lawrence Seaway. Between Long Sault and Ingleside, and in the area of the cemetery on County Road #2, one can see the old Wales village site.

The island facing the cemetery today, upon which St-David's Church was built, was donated by Dr. Stuart. The Union Cemetery wrought iron fence came from the Church cemetery which had been donated by L. G. Wert.

Considering the recent passing away of the last Stuart resident, and its significance in history, the Stuart family has generously offered the home to the Lost Villages Museum.

At this printing, plans to move the home to the Museum are underway.

The Snyder Home

The Snyder home, built by Joseph Eaman of Swiss descendancy more than one hundred eighty years ago, was situated on the Old Post Road near the village of Wales in 1954. As the Snyder home was passed on from one generation to another and has remained in the family, there is no deed of sale. At the time of its construction in 1820, the home was built on one hundred acres of land. The land stretched as far north as, what we know today as, the 401 Highway.

The Snyder home, located on the Old Post Road built in the 1700s for military purposes, was not moved by Ontario Hydro since it sat on higher grounds. Indeed, rather than expropriate the home and the land on which it was situated, only a section of the property considered marsh land and prone to flooding was purchased by Ontario Hydro.

The Old Post Road, located about two miles (3.2 km) from the St. Lawrence River, through the forest, ran from Brockville to Montreal. It made the transport of goods, provisions, and deployment of troops feasible in the event of a military attack on the St. Lawrence River.

Started as a narrow trail through the bush, it expanded to accommodate stagecoach travel and mail from Kingston to Montreal and back. Originally known as the King's Road, it soon was referred to as the Old Post Road. In the last ten years, a section of it has been re-named the Manning Road in reference to the Manning family who originally owned a large section of land obtained through land grants.

On June 25th, 1959, the Hydro Electric Power Commission signed a notice of expropriation of the Snyder property. Then, on April 25, 1960, for the amount of $8,600, the Commission signed a deed of purchase of more than twenty-one acres of the Snyder farmland near Hoople's Creek. The notice of expropriation specified that the land was to be used for the development and the use of the power resources of the International Rapids section of the St. Lawrence River.

This area would then become Crown land as other Crown land south of the new County Road #2 would become. No construction would be allowed on those twenty-one acres.

The architecture of the Snyder home is consistent with the British Regency style of architecture. On its original stone foundation, the storey and a half Snyder home features the low gable roof, the centre door flanked by a tall window on each side with a transom above the door, the wide chimneys, and the veranda popularized between 1810 and 1840.

Since the Seaway construction , the one hundred and five foot (32 m) barn was destroyed and the landscape around the home was changed drastically. The old Highway #2 was relocated and new neighbors moved in, while others left.

The Mary and "Pop" Stuart Home

The Mary and "Pop" Stuart home was the last house moved from Wales. It was built by Arthur "Pop" Stuart for his wife, Mary, during the 1920's.

With its hip-roof, long rectangular form, internal chimney and neo-classic style porch, the Pop Stuart home is an Ontario Cottage style home. It is said that the pattern, used by Charles Manning for the hand made concrete blocks, was fairly common in those days. In fact, a number of homes in the area, from Cornwall to Iroquois, feature various designs of the hand made concrete blocks. However, contrary to the more recent residential construction method of using hollow blocks, those blocks were solid concrete.

This home, owned and moved by Ontario Hydro, was the heaviest house moved during the Seaway Project. Considering that the cargo was extremely heavy, in fact, heavier than had been anticipated, the mover's tires had to be inflated numerous times during the few miles (kilometers) trip to Ingleside. The movers took three days and, for everyone's safety, had to be accompanied by an Ontario Provincial Police constable.

Although the village of Wales grew slowly over the years and had changed name from Dickinson's Landing Station in 1860, it remained mostly a small farming community until the Seaway project. At the time of the Seaway construction, Wales had shrunken down to only a few families and the "Mocassin" had ceased to exist.

The small hamlets of Woodlands and Santa Cruz, south west of Wales and west of Dickinson's Landing, were mostly farmland dating back to the early Loyalist settlers, in 1784. Woodlands was known for its timber used by the steamers on the river. Woodlands had two general stores, a church, and a post office. The Campbell's (Camp Belle) cottages, on the river, catered to tourists.

During the construction of the project, the village of Wales disappeared completely along with the hamlets of Woodlands and Santa Cruz. One of the most westerly islands of the Long Sault Parkway, named Woodlands, commemorates the lost hamlet of Woodlands. It has a campground and a picnic area which welcomes day or overnight visitors.

The home remained vacant for a short while after its move prior to being lived in by the Acres family for twenty years. The present owners take great pride in the Stuart home and appreciate its beauty and unique historic features.

The Warren-Rice Home

The Warren-Rice home, as it was called, was the largest residential wooden frame structure moved to Ingleside during the Seaway Project. It had been built at the north end of the village of Wales for Fred Warren and Ida Wert in the 1880s. Pictures show that, while in Wales, the home looked grandiose. It had a front yard surrounded by a cement block fence flanked centrally by two urns raised on posts. Both urns have been preserved and are still in front of the home today.

The Warren-Rice home was moved to Maxwell Street, in Ingleside, before the flood of 1958. Although the home had an open porch with three columns supporting a roof, after the move the porch was enclosed.

Its butternut interior wood trim, built from butternut trees on the Wales property, its original swinging door to the dining room, its leaded glass on either side of the fireplace, and its Mille Roches pottery tiles above the fireplace have been impeccably preserved. It is reported that the home won an architectural award at the 1887 New York Sate Fair.

The leaf pattern on the stairs' railing posts were carved by a shipwright from Maine. The stairs lead the visitors to a large upstairs area divided into four bedrooms, two of which have private salons, and one small nursery bedroom with two cedar wood closets.

Originally called Smartville, then Dickinson's Landing Station, the old village was renamed Wales in honor of the Prince of Wales. While passing through to experience a steamship cruise through the Rapids in 1860, his Royal Highness, Albert Edward, the nineteen year old Prince of Wales, questioned the name of the village or its lack thereof. Interpreted as an invitation for change, his comments were sufficient to cause the renaming of the small village to Wales.

Wales remained a small community until the appearance of the Grand Trunk Railway in 1856. Visitors who wanted to shoot the Long Sault Rapids on steamboats used to travel on the Grand Trunk to Wales, and through Dickinson's Landing situated on the shores of the St. Lawrence River, south of Wales.

Aside from the train which kept the village alive, Wales was largely a small farming community. There were two general stores, one owned and operated by Ransom and Trimble, and the other by Albert L. Feader, a hotel, the Henry Laflamme's Barber Shop, St-David's Anglican Church, the S.S. No. 6 school, the Wales Continuation School, a feedmill, an egg grading station, and a poultry farm built by L. G. Wert. During difficult depression years, the L. G. Wert egg hatchery provided much needed work and income for many residents.

The home is fondly remembered for having housed the Warren-Rice Insurance Company for many years. The company provided insurance for life, accident, fire, farm, liability, and burglary.

Since 1999, as a unique inn, it has been welcoming tourists and visitors under the name "Nightingale House". The present owners, Lesley and Stuart O'Gorman, have brought it back to its grandiose days and have transformed it into a Bed and Breakfast Inn, known for its warm hospitality and exceptional Victorian afternoon teas.

It is the front door of the Nightingale House which is featured on the cover page of the book.

The Wert Home

It is reported that the Werts, who settled this area after the American Revolution, were brothers, Conrad and John, who joined the Loyalist King's Royal Regiment of New York in May, 1780. Records show that the surname was variously spelled Wart, Wort, Wartt and, more commonly, Weart, or Wert.

The Wearts, as did many of their neighbors in the Mohawk Valley, had come from the Palatine states of Germany and had settled in America, in the early 1700's, at the invitation of Britain's protestant Queen Anne, who granted them crown land in the colony of New York. Although the majority were Lutheran Germans, who had been persecuted for their religious beliefs in Europe, the British Government had been sympathetic.

The Regiment, formed in Quebec during the American Revolution, was made up mostly of farmers, who owned or rented land in the Albany area of New York. They were loyal to the British Crown and to their local leader and commanding officer, Sir John Johnson. At the end of the war, they travelled through Sorel, Quebec, on their way westward up the St. Lawrence River to Cornwall, where John drew two hundred acres on Lot 9, concession 2 of Osnabruck Township, as well as several one hundred acre lots in the sixth and seventh concessions of the same township.

After John Weart and his wife, Dorothy Eaman, cleared the land, they probably built a small log home, followed by a larger log or frame home, close to the front of their property. In the 1840s, judging by the external architecture and design of the home, John's son, Conrad, built this large square brick home in the neo-classical design with a number of well preserved features which can be seen today.

The historic home has some of the original bubble glass windows, the fan-shape transom above the front door with the side-light doorway, the nine foot ceilings, and the burlap cloth patterns in the bricks. The unique hardwood-patterned floor of the west parlour was installed in the 1930s, and was not part of the original house carpentry. The front porch section was added in 1934.

The home was successively owned by John's heirs - Conrad Weart, George Weart, Corrie E. Wert and Harry Shaver-Wert. In 1957, although it was planned for the home not to be flooded, Harry Shaver-Wert believed that the structure would be too close to the newly created shores of the St. Lawrence River. Indeed, it was foreseen that when the waters would rise the home might suffer continual basement flooding, water damage, and permanent dampness. Therefore, Harry Shaver-Wert sold the home to Ontario Hydro with the intended purpose of seeing its destruction to make way for the project.

After the flooding, it was found that the waters did not affect the home as seriously as first thought. Moreover, the flood of 1958 transformed the land surrounding old Hoople Creek into the present day Hoople Creek Bay and a section of the front lawn of the Wert home into a picturesque waterfront setting.

Following a brief life as a stopover home, it was purchased by the present owners, in 1960, who have taken great pride in owning the Wert home.

The Wert Home Front Door

At the end of the War of Independence, soldiers and their families fled north either to Nova Scotia, New Brunswick, or to the British Province of Quebec. Canada, as we know it today, was known as the British Province of Quebec with its French Seigneurial system of Government and land ownership. The Constitutional Act which created a division between Upper and Lower Canada, passed in 1791, ensured that grantees had full title to their land under British rule. Prior to that law a short version of the land grant was issued with mention of the "Seigneurie" (as in the Stuart land grant) in the text.

Under the new Act, a long version of land grant was developed through the Upper Canada Registry Office with a number of clarifications as well as conditions added to the text. It was printed on a form which allowed the Auditor General or his Representative to fill in by hand the pertinent information related to the grantee. The form was printed on the presses of the Upper Canada Gazette in Niagara-on-the-Lake by Louis Roy, a Quebecer, who arrived with Lieutenant-Governor of Upper Canada, John Graves Simcoe, in 1793. The Land Grant documents were printed on a parchment-type paper folded a number of times. They were then woven through, with a red tape, to which the King's red wax seal was attached, before being delivered to the owner. Generally speaking they included 6 sections: Salutations, description of the granted land, reservation of certain rights, responsibilities of the owner, default conditions, and signatures.

The Wert family, through John Wart Senior, received a land grant for services rendered to King George III. The Land Grant reads in part:

Upper Canada   Peter Russell, President
GEORGE THE THIRD, by the Grace of GOD of Great-Britain, France and Ireland King, defender of the faith, and fo forth, to all to whom thefe prefents f h a l l   c o m e ,   G R E E T I N G S :
....DO GIVE and GRANT onto John Wart Senr be the same more or lefs, being compofed of lot the E half of Lot No 32 6 concefsion lot No 11 & 30 7ᵗʰ concefsion and situate, lying and being in the Township of Osnabruck

aforesaid, in the county of Stormont and Eastern District of our province aforesaid, ... which faid five hundred Acres of Land, are butted and bounded, or may be otherwife known as follows (that is to fay). Beginning at the part in front of 6ᵗʰ conc., marked 31/31. - Then North 24 West, 105 Chains, 27 Links, then South 66 West, 9 chains, 50 links then South 24 East, 105 Chains, 27 Links, then North 66 East, 9 Chains, 50 Links, to the place of beginning...
....IN RESPECT of the land to be hereby granted, now know ye, that we caufed an allottment, or appropriation of Seventy One Acres & Three Sevenths to be m a d e   i n   t h e   L o t s   N o   1 1 .   8 .   &   9ᵗʰ   C o n c e f s i o n . Being in the proportion of one to feven of the lands fo hereby granted, as and for a referve, and to and for the fole ufe, benefit and fupport of a proteftant clergy. TO HAVE and TO HOLD the faid parcel or tract of land to him the faid John Wart Senr and his heirs and affigns forever, faving neverthelefs to us, our heirs and fuccefors all mines of gold, filver, copper, tin, lead, iron and coal ...and faving and referving to us our heirs and fucceffors, all white pine trees that fhall, or may now, or hereafter grow, or be growing on any part of the faid parcel or tract of land hereby granted as aforesaid. ....Provided alfo that the faid John Wart Senr his heirs and affigns fhall and do within three years erect and build, or caufe to be erected and built, some part of the faid parcel or tract of land a good and fufficient dwelling house, he the said John Wart Senr and his heirs shall come into paffeffion and tenure ... within twelve months next after his, her or their entry into, and poffeffion of the fame, take the oaths prefcribed by law, before fome one of the magiftrates of our faid Province; and a certificate of fuch oaths having been fo taken fhall caufe to be recorded in the fecretary's office in the faid Province: IN DEFAULT of all or any of which faid conditions, limitations and reftrictions, this said grant, and every thing herein contained, fhall be, and WE do hereby declare the fame to be null and void, to all intents and purpofes whatfoever; and the land hereby granted, and every part and parcel thereof, fhall revert to, and become vested in us, our Heirs and Succeffors in like manner as if the fame had never been granted; .....GIVEN under the great Seal of our Province of Upper Canada:

WITNESS the Honorable Peter Rufsell our Administrator of the Government of our faid Province, this twenty-seventh day of September in the year of our Lord, one thoufand feven hundred and nine seven and thirty seventh or our reign. P.R.
Ww. B. Peters Afsist Sec'y

The O'Dette Home

The O'Dette home was situated on three-quarters of an acre in front of Highway #2, on the west half of Lot 13, first concession, in Dickinson's Landing. Records show that the property was registered in 1835. It was a large, multi-gabled frame house, with a barn and a terraced garden. Two hard maple trees had been named Harry and Arthur after their planters. Although there were few trees on the property, it was referred to as the "Orchards". In 1946, a lean-to addition was built at the rear to form the kitchen and an added stairway led to the basement.

In 1957, one hundred and twenty-two years after its construction, the O'Dette home was moved to Ingleside on Dickinson's Drive. The Dunlop family's sun porch, built by Ellison Henry, carpenter, and the Jack Geddes's garage joined the O'Dette home in Ingleside. Following its move to Ingleside, the Edmund Murphy family, as well as the Rice family, owned the home successively.

Attachment to the land, as well as a great fondness for one's own lost village, has inspired numbers of local authors to document their unique histories. Writing to share fond memories, as well as to remember former neighbors and friends, has been a means for local historians to transmit their memories of old to the next generation. Indeed, to honor those pioneers and community leaders, Leonard O'Dette, along with many other writers since 1958, have produced works of historic value. Through their work, fictitious and not, their humourous anecdotes, personal experiences, and candid comments, memories of the old villages are recalled. Videotapes, books, historic plaques, movies, videos, and photographs have documented the lives of the lost riverside communities and its people.

Moreover, a number of local artists have depicted beautiful areas of the landscape and the local homes on their canvases. Historical Societies have arisen, in the intervening years, with the objective to document and preserve the unique history and rich archives of the founding communities. It is reported that affection for the St. Lawrence River has even motivated a family to name a child born in 1954, Lawrence.

Through his writing, Leonard O'Dette introduced us to Dickinson's Landing. Situated south of Wales, the lost village of Dickinson's Landing was in the Township of Osnabruck and County of Stormont. It was located east of Hoople's Creek, at the head of the Long Sault Rapids, facing the St. Lawrence River, and approximately six miles (9.6 km) from Cornwall. The Cornwall Canal ended at the east end of Dickinson's Landing.

It is said that in 1669, Lasalle, who had left Lachine in search of furs and souls, established a trading post and a resting place at the head of the Rapids. It was Barnabas Dickenson (Barnabus Dickinson), born in Massachusetts in 1783, who founded the small community in 1812. As a stage coach operator he began the first Montreal-Kingston mail service. Barnabas died of cholera in Cornwall in 1832. The light house situated at the western tip of the Cornwall canal in the village of Dickinson's Landing guided the river pilots for years until it was moved to the Upper Canada Village Museum in 1958.

Aside from a few renovations, the O'Dette home, as it was known, now stands in Ingleside. Sophia Cheresna, who has lived in the home for fourteen years, enjoys its long history and many of its unique features such as the original narrow stairwell leading upstairs, its wide baseboards, and its south side sun porch.

The Shaver Home

The Shaver home was originally situated in the west-end of the picturesque village of Dickinson's Landing on part of the two hundred acre lot granted to Jacob Eaman' son, Nicholas, in 1833. The large home, on the summit of one of the Landing's hills, was surrounded by a paneled wood-and-iron-shaped fence. In 1867 and 1881, sections of the lot were sold to Catherine Waterman as well as to George Nicholas and his wife, Nancy Eaman. In 1910, James Herman Shaver bought the property.

James Herman Shaver was born on December 16, 1839, in Osnabruck Township. In March 1867, James married Theresa Wood, daughter of Colonel John Roger Wood, United Empire Loyalist descendant.

Roger, born on May 18, 1808, James H. Shaver's father-in-law, transformed the small farm forge into a successful foundry employing men from the surrounding communities. It is most probable that James H. Shaver, a contractor, was employed at the foundry. It is reported that while at the height of his prosperity, John Roger owned stage coaches and a carriage and pair, unique in Osnabruck. This enterprise prospered for twenty years until a fire broke out and destroyed the small business as well as John's home. John Roger Wood was made Lieutenant Colonel in command of the Second Battalion of Stormont Militia during the 1837 Rebellion.

In order to avoid the numerous rapids between Montreal and Lake Ontario, river travellers used to load, and unload, their goods onto boats and coaches a number of times along the way. Indeed, prior to access to the canals, the transport of people and goods required portage along the banks of the St. Lawrence River from Montreal to the Great Lakes. Near the Long Sault Rapids, from east to west and vice-versa, all travelers and steamer ships had to make a stopover at Dickinson's Landing. Early footpath passages progressed from corduroy roads, to gravelled ones, to limited pavement during the 1920s.

Moreover, the unpaved roads, used to avoid rapids and treacherous water, made transport and travel a challenge. The time necessary for the transferring manoeuvres added to the difficulties of the journey. A trip on the St. Lawrence River was indeed an adventure as well as a timely and costly business enterprise. The stage coach business flourished. Entrepreneurs of the era saw an opportunity in the shipping trade which evolved into a business known as "forwarding". Hotels and inns grew in strategic areas where boats would make stopovers.

A number of steamships, such as the Rapids King, Queen, and Prince became well known in the riverside communities. In 1860, Albert Edward, Prince of Wales, later to become King Edward VII, was the guest of honor for the grand opening of the Victoria Bridge in Montreal. It is reported that he enjoyed a ride on the newly built Grand Trunk Railway to the Wales station. Colonel John Roger Wood, in his best coach, met the Prince at the station, and brought him to Dickinson's Landing from where the Prince continued his trip on to Montreal by steamer over the Long Sault Rapids.

In 1920, one year before his wife's death and eighteen months before his own death, on October 29, 1921, James Herman Shaver sold the property as well as the right-of-way along both sides of Hoople's Creek.

In 1957, the home was moved by Ontario Hydro to Ingleside and was rented to Hydro workers. In 1966, Donald Gregor Williamson, who was renting the property from Ontario Hydro, purchased it.

While a number of renovations were done over the years, the home's interior has retained many of its original features. Moreover, some of the exterior unique characteristics have been restored.

It is with a great sense of pride that the present owners strive to maintain the home's historic integrity.

The Snetsinger Home

Descendants of United Empire Loyalists, Mathias Snetsinger (1790 - 1855) his wife, Margaret Cline (1794 - 1873), brothers, John Snetsinger and Alex Snetsinger, left their marks in the small communities of Dickinson's Landing and Moulinette.

As a port of entry with a customs official and its proximity with the Grand Trunk Railway, the village of Dickinson's Landing, situated east of Hoople's Creek, thrived until 1842. In the 1857 Canada Directory, it is reported that Dickinson's Landing had a population of five hundred. Built on the water, the village had a sawmill, a soap factory, a tannery, a potash factory, a tailor shop, an undertaker, a bakery, a butcher, a number of hotels, a post office, some general stores, schools, and churches. In the stage coach era, it is said that Dickinson's Landing's prosperity was nearly equal to that of Cornwall.

In 1916, John Snetsinger, with his wife, Edith Uella Forsythe (1893 - 1949), bought and developed the successful Sweet Briar Cheese factory in Dickinson's Landing until 1941. At the Eastern Ontario Dairy Convention, John was a repeated prize winner for his superior cheese. In fact, he won three gold medals for producing 100% Grade "A" cheese for three consecutive years. His brother, Alex, purchased the Black River Factory and developed it into a thriving business. They both graduated from the Eastern Dairy School in Kingston. Alex became an important leader in the movement to obtain a substantial rise in the price of cheese.

John and Alex were the second and first sons of John J. Snetsinger and Margaret Scott. The Snetsinger home, on King Street and old Highway #2, was facing the St. Lawrence River before 1954. It was situated across the road from the factory. The large two-storey brick home, built during the last quarter of the nineteenth century, had two chimneys and featured four large front windows as well as side windows, equivalent in size to the front door. As well, a two storey, glassed-in veranda, covering the entire front of the home, added character to the building.

It is reported that the home was temporarily used by the militia during a skirmish at the Creek. Moreover, at one time or another the home served as a funeral home, a post office, and a Colonial Coach Line stop. In the wing at the rear of the home, a seamstress was available for repairs.

John's factory was known for being the best equipped cheese factory in the area. In addition to cheddar cheese, it manufactured whey butter and curd. Cheese making started in early April and ceased in late November of each year. The factory was equipped with an ice chamber, curing and storage areas, and an office. It is said that, in 1916, the factory produced more than 210,000 pounds (95,454 kg) of cheese. Like many cheese factory owners, John Snetsinger sold his product through the Cornwall Cheese and Butter Board. On a weekly basis, one hundred and forty boxes of cheese were shipped through the Montreal port to England.

Harold Snetsinger, son of John, and his wife, Laura Windle, owned and operated a general store at Dickinson's Landing. The store was housed in a two bedroom cottage with a sitting room, a kitchen and a side porch. The residence and the store were built, owned, and operated by Wilbert Kyer in the early 40s. The ten feet by twenty feet (3 m by 6 m) store faced Highway #2.

During the seaway relocation, while the home was sold and was moved north to the village of Finch, Hydro offered the Snetsingers a home in Ingleside from which to temporarily operate a general store. After ten months, the Snetsingers moved their store to the new Ingleside shopping centre where they continued to operate and serve the community for twenty years. John Snetsinger's two-storey home and factory in Dickinson's Landing were destroyed to make way for the St. Lawrence Seaway and Power project.

The Kerr Home

The Kerr home, in Farran's Point, had come to be known as "Buckingham Palace" because of its large size. The family home was situated on a corner lot facing the St. Lawrence River. Quite unusual in its construction, the home was built not only on a corner lot but turned the corner at a 40 degree angle and housed a general store at its east end. In reference to its rambling construction and conspicuous tower, the brick home, in its bustling days, was a community center where business deals and social events were part of the daily life.

Originally from Morrisburg, the Moyle family had transformed the place into living quarters for the family, in 1940, and reserved an area for the store and a garage. At the time of the Seaway, while the upper floor had been modified into apartments, the Moyle family was still living at "Buckingham Palace".

Belvederes, or cupolas, on the crown of the house roof, common in Ontario homes, were designed to add light in bedrooms situated under the roof, or on the second floor of the home. In addition, they were quite common in homes situated near the water, as is with the Kerr home, as a means to look out on the water and monitor the shipping activity.

Farran's Point was named after Jacob Farrand, a Lieutenant in the King's Royal regiment. The village was situated about eight miles from Cornwall and faced small rapids, which would later be named after the Lieutenant. The one-mile canal, which was built during the mid-nineteenth century to avoid the rapids and the three-foot drop in water level, would also be named Farran's Point Canal.

In addition to the Farrans, the Kerrs were also instrumental in the development of the early community of Farran's Point. Originally from Ireland, the Kerr family settled at Farran's Point, where they opened a general store, owned and operated some farms as well as a saw mill and a grist mill. Two children of the family, Joseph and George, served in the Legislative Assembly.

Joseph was born in the County of Fermanagh, Ireland, in 1849, and, as a young man, was employed as a conductor by the Grand Trunk Railway. He was the son of William Kerr and Margaret Smith. In 1879, Joseph Kerr was elected Member of Parliament for Stormont.

His brothers, Thomas, William, and George, with their mother, joined Joseph at Farran's Point, township of Osnabruck, where they developed a flourishing mercantile business - the Kerr Brothers. There were branch stores situated in Aultsville and Wales as well.

George, the youngest of the family, who was also born in Ireland, married, in 1872, Margery Ann Sutherland, a grand-daughter of Colonel Walter Sutherland of the King's Regiment of New York, and an original settler of Lancaster Township. George was elected a member of the Legislative Assembly, in 1905, and died in 1913.

"Buckingham Palace" was destroyed to make way for the St. Lawrence Project.

The Sheets Home

The Sheets home, which was situated in Farran's Point, was moved to Ingleside on Maxwell Street in 1957. It was built by David Empey and William Hollister sometime between 1925 and 1926. The Sheets home exterior is made of stucco, a fairly rare material in Upper Canada. Use of that material as an exterior finish for a home started around 1830. Uncommon in Upper Canada, it was seen in Toronto as early as 1835.

The home's partly-covered front porch creates an umbrage, or recessed area, precursor of the Upper Canada verandas and covered porches.

A young man named Farrand, born in Belfast, Ireland, of Huguenot descent, is credited for the naming of the village of Farran's Point. It was, indeed, on Jacob Farrand's land granted to him as a Lieutenant in the King's Regiment that Farran's Point was built. In the 1800's, when the Farran's Point canal and locks were built, the government granted power generated by the rapids to Charles Curtis Farran. He used it to run his carding, his saw, and his shingles mills.

The Post Office was also operated by C.C. Farran.

The small riverside village was situated between the hamlet of Woodland and the village of Aultsville along the Highway #2. Although the community had a number of small businesses, it depended on the canal for employment and prosperity.

The "Point" village had a number of mills, general stores, a hotel, two churches, a blacksmith shop, a bake shop, a hat factory, a wheelwright shop, a school, a tin shop, a dance pavilion near a much enjoyed park along the St. Lawrence River at lock 22, and a station of the Grand Trunk train which brought mail daily. It was also known for its ice-cutting activities in the winter.

Although Farran's Point made efforts to expand, it remained a small village with a population of one hundred fifty, in 1857, and two hundred, in 1879.

While the canal and lock #22 are underwater today, they are a stone's throw from Farran Park created in 1958 as a part of the rehabilitation program of the Seaway and Power project.

The present owners have lived in the home since the Seaway project. Although they have added a sunroom at the rear of the home, they have also taken care to preserve some of its unique features such as the living room hardwood patterned floor and wood trim.

The Ault Home

The Ault home was built by a United Empire Loyalist, Captain Nicholas N. Ault of the Stormont Militia, more than two hundred years ago in the village of Aultsville. The home had billeted a number of "Redcoats" during the raids.

The home was not only the birthplace of five generations of the Ault family, but was the Ault family homestead. Captain Nicholas N. Ault, who had served in the war of 1812 to 1814 and in the Fenian raids, had a number of descendants who were instrumental in the creation and the development of the village of Aultsville.

Nicholas N's son, Nicholas J., dealing in the mercantile business, damned the creek, built a sawmill near the river, and shipped lumber to Montreal. The general store, which he built, was later managed by Samuel, also a son of Nicholas N. Other brothers, Isaiah and Simeon, expanded the family's mercantile business under the name I. R. Ault Bros. Ltd.. Faced with flourishing success, the brothers were able to expand and build a couple of other homes in the village of Aultsville.

Isaiah was born in Osnabruck in 1824, and died in 1889, after serving his community as Postmaster in 1854, Reeve of the Township of Osnabruck and finally as Warden for the Counties of Stormont in 1881. It is said that due to Isaiah's interest in local affairs, the village of Aultsville became a most attractive rural village in the counties.

Samuel, married to Catherine Loucks, daughter of John W. Loucks, went on to become Warden in 1852 and MPP from 1861 to 1867. He was elected a Member of Parliament from 1867 to 1872, and served during the first five years of the Dominion of Canada.

D'Arcy Ault, son of Samuel Ault, was born in the village of Aultsville in 1842. He graduated from Upper Canada College and pursued his medical studies at McGill University, in Montreal. After his graduation, in 1868, he practiced as a family physician for many years.

Originally called Charlesville (reason unknown), Aultsville was later renamed in honor of Samuel Ault. The small village of Aultsville prospered because of his contribution to the community.

Since Nicholas N's military service, there have been a number of soldiers in the Ault family. Up to the time of the Seaway, a descendant of Nicholas N, Gordon Ault, was stationed in England with the RCAF. In 1954, his mother, Flora McArthur of Williamsburg, was living in the home.

The home's original interior had been modified over the years by the succeeding Ault generations. However, its brick exterior along with its large windows suggest its former grand living.

The destruction of the lost village of Aultsville, which had been built around the Ault home, included the destruction of the Ault homestead.

The McLaren Home

The Lena and Connie McLaren home, moved from Aultsville to Ingleside, was built in the 1880's. The McLaren home has a number of attractive features such as a one-and-a-half-storey, shallow pitched roof, and high walls. It is an ell-shaped home featuring the gable end turned toward the front of the house, typical of the side-hall plan home building traditions introduced in the 1820's. Thus, the front door is on the shorter side of the rectangular house. The wider facade of the ell shape home also features a side wing which, traditionally, was the kitchen area. The second floor on the left side was added between the original construction period, and before 1929.

The original home exterior was entirely made of bricks. Unbeknownst to the present owners, during a recent upgrade to the house, it was discovered that the exterior was, indeed, built of two courses of bricks. It is suspected that the bricks used to build the McLaren home came from the Elliott Pottery and Brickyard factory, in Aultsville, a short distance west of Dickinson's Landing. Our pioneers used an extra layer of uncured bricks, as insulation.

Due to its geographic situation, Aultsville was reported to have grown from its 120 inhabitants in 1846, to a population of 300, in 1871, and 400 in 1879. Meandering along the village of Aultsville, the Aultsville Creek provided sufficient water power to supply a number of mills in the area. In addition, the river provided easy access to transportation and, as well, it was a great source of clay for pottery and brickwork. Indeed, William and John Elliott developed a brickyard and pottery factory near the creek.

It is believed, although not confirmed in the records, that the bricks used to build a number of homes in this area also come from the Elliott Pottery factory in Aultsville.

Clay from the river bed became the source of raw material for bricks used to build homes. The factory used the soil from the St. Lawrence River from the mid-1800's to the turn of the century for the manufacture of bricks, pottery, and other household wares.

Aultsville was once a thriving small town which included elementary and secondary schools, and three churches. Some of the industries were the Edwards Cheese factory and the Melody Acres poultry farm. The Jarvis and Shaver General store with a grist mill was transformed into an egg-grading station in the 1930's.

Other enterprises were the Dafoe General Store, the Markell bakeshop, the Moss barber shop, the Borden's Chateau Cheese division plant, the Empey ferry crossing to Louisville Landing on the American side, the Riverview Hotel, the Elliott Pottery and Brickyard factory, the Wells automobile dealership, and a branch of the Bank of Montreal. There were other flourishing industries such as a tannery, a butcher shop, a millinery shop, a customs and immigration office, and the Grand Trunk station, ensuring daily mail delivery. Moreover, it is reported that in 1869, other Aultsville commodities were lumber and cordwood.

The famous Dr. Samuel Alan Hickey, son of John Allan Hickey, and Dr. Edward D'Arcy Ault, son of Samuel Ault, both practiced medicine here during the late 1800's. Dr. Lyell Brown, also fondly remembered, was the last doctor to serve his Aultsville community as well as the families on the American shores.

Due to their weight, only a small number of brick homes were moved during the Seaway Project.

The Froats Home

Built in Aultsville by Michael Urias Cook, circa 1845, the home of Edwin and Doris Froats had been previously owned by the Orval Beckstead family and, before that, by the descendants of its builder.

In 1957, it was moved to the Upper Canada Village Museum and restored to the 1850 period. As the Museum had moved a number of homes from the flooded areas and recreated life in a typical village during the Confederation period, the Froats's home was given the fictional designation of being a doctor's home.

Prior to the arrival of military surgeons and university trained medical doctors, medicine was largely a matter of home remedies, common sense, and aboriginal traditional medicine. Until the universities of Toronto, Queen's, and McGill set up programs, graduates from American and European medical schools migrated to Upper Canada and set up their practices.

Although the Froats' home was never a doctor's home, its layout was suitable for a fictional village physician. In the early days of the Village, interpreters used to refer to Dr. Patrick Keogh, a Dublin graduate, as the local physician, but, more recently, the local doctor is Doctor John Macdonald, a graduate of Queen's Medical school in Kingston.

The home's exposed brick exterior paired with its original partly covered front veranda are no longer there today. The style of other such homes in the area served as inspiration for the restoration of the neo-Grecian (neo-classic) home. A concave roof and trellis support for the front verandah were common in the 1850's. In addition, the desire to bring the garden closer to the home precipitated the development of wooden treillage as a replacement of classic columns around verandas, in Upper Canada and, in other areas in Ontario. Trellis work allowed vines to grow and created desired shading. Treillage of complex straight wooden bar patterns as well as elaborate ornamental Victorian curves, increased in popularity.

While the circular window motif was popular in many early homes in Upper Canada, the ellipse motif on the second storey window was a typical neo-classic architectural feature.

The Froats' home has two side wings, similar to the design of Crysler Hall, reminiscent of the eighteenth century desire for balanced proportion. The wings, often referred to as tails, were the preferred location for the kitchens. However, the kitchen of the Froats's home is in the back of the central section of the house. As a home of the 1840s, it has no fireplaces, but is heated by stoves and a system of pipes.

Originally, doctors did not have an "office" in their own homes, but rather, a "study". They made house-calls exclusively. Later on, the study became an office. The east wing of the home contains the doctor's study and displays some of the equipment of his profession. Doctors often prepared their own pharmaceutical preparations. According to medical record books, itch ointments, eyewash, and purgatives were most frequently prescribed.

The stenciled floor in the large bedroom has survived the years of wear and is an exceptional example of a family's creative resourcefulness.

Thus, the home serves to honor the country doctor's devotion and generosity toward his patients.

The Merkle Home

The Merkle home, built in 1818, is a Georgian style home. It was situated east of Morrisburg, along the St. Lawrence River in the area of Aultsville called "The Churches".

The early Loyalists built two basic types of homes: the Cape Cod and the Georgian. The Cape Cod cottage was an unpretentious vernacular homestead usually facing south, was one-and-a-half-storey high, had a single chimney, often had a shingled gable roof, and clapboard exterior walls. It often had windows with nine panes of glass in the upper sash and six in the lower sash, a small entry, a steep staircase, and an attic.

On the other hand, the Georgian home was usually quite large, ostentatious, and had its origins in the European architecture. It often reflected the owners influence and affluence. Its links to the Georgian England made it a symbol of British presence in the new country. Loyalists, or home owners with strong British ties, preferred this style of architecture. Its name, "Georgian", comes from the first four British rulers named "George" who reigned between 1714 and 1830. This style, rooted in the classical design principles of Rome and Greece, was brought in by a large number of masons, framers and joiners who emigrated from England during the eighteenth century. Thus, it was as part of their cultural baggage that the Loyalists brought the Georgian style home from the United States.

Symmetry and regularity are its typical features. The Georgian interpretation of those classical styles produced buildings exhibiting calm, order, and good taste. The architecture style is refined, formal, and takes its origin in the Greek, Roman Renaissance, and Post-Renaissance architects of the sixteenth century, known as the Palladians.

The Georgian home had two storeys, five bays, and a wide entrance in the centre of the long exterior wall. If the Loyalist home had decorative features, they were concentrated around the front door and sometimes around the ground floor windows. The elliptical fan transom set above the wider door with side lights, a Palladian motif, became a characteristic of the home referred to as the Loyalist home.

At one time owned by the Merkle family, the home was the property of John Pliny Crysler's family during the mid-nineteenth century. As the son of John Crysler and Nancy Loucks, United Empire Loyalists, John P. who was born on February 26, 1801, had received a land grant on February 2, 1825. There he built his home. John Pliny Crysler died in Morrisburg on April 7, 1881.

During the 1920's and 1930's, it served as a Bed and Breakfast. In 1956, the home was owned by the Lee Casselman family. At the time of the Seaway construction, there was a debate about whether to move this home or the Cook's home to Upper Canada Village Museum. The present owners saw the distinct possibility of its destruction and, in an inspired move, decided to save it. They purchased it from Ontario Hydro and arranged for its relocation. In the spirit of the pioneers before them, they rebuilt it themselves with a minimum of assistance. The home has retained its original beauty and unique features through their masterful restoration.

Considering its weight, windows, doors, and almost sixty thousand bricks were removed. During the reconstruction, it was discovered that the home originally had three courses of bricks, the middle one having traces of damage by fire. The large entrance welcomes the visitors into a hall on each side of which is a living room and a dining room. The family bedrooms are on the second floor.

The interior woodwork finish has been preserved and many of the original features of the homes are still intact.

The Ontario Hydro Home

It is not known who built this home, nor is it clear when it was built or who the early owners were. But during the seaway construction, it was situated in the area known as "The Churches" between old Morrisburg and Aultsville. Not unlike a good number of homes bought by Ontario Hydro in 1954, this home, was moved to Riverside Heights. It was still in the hands of Ontario Hydro six years after the end of the project, in 1958. It had been rented out while waiting to be sold.

Riverside Heights, situated between Ingleside and Morrisburg, west of the Upper Canada Village Museum, was created to receive twenty-nine homes from the Williamsburg Township villages affected by the flood of 1958. For the displaced families, the new site traded the view of the river for a view of the forest.

As many displaced families had owned farms along the St. Lawrence River, the lots were made larger to accommodate new gardens. Those families who wished to continue farming had to move to other areas. Although each new town had its own town centre development plan in which residents participated, the final outline for Riverside Heights was designed to replicate the original strip villages along the river. It was determined that each home would have a street access while every third or fourth lot would be ell-shaped, thus larger.

In the style of the Ontario Vernacular, the home is a regional adaptation of the Gothic style home. Indeed, the vernacular home was designed as a direct response to the availability of materials, local conditions, and observations made by the builders of the time. The Gothic home was often a one and a half storey wood frame home with side gables and one central gable with a dormer over the front entrance. Sheathed in clapboard and covered with a saltbox style roof with the predominant ridge well toward the front of the house, the home is often locally referred to as the Harrowsmith home.

The second floor dormer was designed to provide additional space for a bathroom and to add light to the second storey area. The home's symmetrical plan was strongly influenced by the Colonial Georgian style characterized by a balanced facade of three to seven rectangular windows, evenly spaced, on either side of a central front door.

Popularized in Eastern Ontario was the addition of one or more side wings or tails to a home and which had a number of functions. Many tails, which could be attached in a row to the home, were used for various purposes. In the winter, the cook-stove was used in the kitchen, while in the summer, it was often moved to either a summer kitchen or the airy wood-shed extending from the kitchen space. Single-flue brick chimneys accommodated pipes.

The present owners, along with other family members, bought a number of homes in Riverside Heights, in 1965, and continue to enjoy the friendly, small, riverside community environment.

The Lawrence Home

Life for the riverside communities was mainly defined by activities on land such as farming, and on the river as boating, swimming, and fishing. Equally important, the river provided economic growth and wealth to the small villages along the shores. As the river was made more navigable by the construction of the canals west of Iroquois to Montreal, the vessels increased in size, depth (draft), width, and ability to carry heavier cargos. Canoes, batteaux, canallers, steam boats, lakers, and ocean-going vessels succeeded each other as means of transport of people and goods.

Until 1954, ships had the option of using the canals up and down the river or descending across the numerous rapids, from Kingston to Montreal. Navigating along the rapids required knowledge of the twists and turns of the river as well as the skill to move the vessels through safe waters. Ship captains used the services of pilots to safely maneuver their ships through rough and turbulent rapids. It is reported that a number of river pilots, born in the Dickinson's Landing area, emerged as talented and skilled steamboat captains of the St. Lawrence River.

It is said that river pilotage was passed on from father to son, for generations. Ever since Champlain wrote about the native mastery of the river, the native Indians continued to pilot the numerous river boats, including the luxurious Rapids Queen and Rapids Prince of the 1800s, cruise ships of yesteryear. A legendary native Indian named John Rice, fondly known as Big John, from the Kahnasatake Indian reserve south of Montreal, initiated Edouard Ouellette on river pilotage. Edward, in turn, taught his nephew, Edouard Joseph Ouellette.

In 1903, at the age of 17, young Edouard started pilotage with the Richelieu and the Ontario Navigating Companies. By 1916, he was a captain working for Canada Steamship Lines. His expertise was undoubtedly much appreciated by the travelers as it was common belief that to have a native pilot at the helm was assurance of safety.

Parallel to the advent of the Seaway, Edouard Joseph Ouellette's death, in 1963, marked the end of an era for the rapids pilots. Captain J. P. Stephenson, who piloted boats through the rapids for fifty years was the last pilot to run the rapids. The lighthouse which guided pilots for decades at the western tip of the Cornwall canal was moved to the Upper Canada Village Museum in 1957.

Today, the tradition of father-son pilotage is still alive. Born prior to the canal construction of the mid-eighteenth century, this expert skill has been dramatically transformed by standards, regulations, government policies, associations, and guilds. Moreover, the construction of the Seaway, the newly built larger ships, and the international influence on the expanding shipping industry transformed river pilotage of the St. Lawrence River into a profession. Pilots are licensed for navigating certain sections of the river.

Ault Island, situated between Morrisburg, at the west, and Ingleside at the east, and south of County Road #2 facing the St. Lawrence River, was created, in 1954, to receive some cottages from Sheek's Island. Today, there are few cottages left on the island and very few of the original owners still live there.

In 1980, as a number of lots along the river, at the east end of the island, still remained vacant, Ontario Hydro sold them.

John Lawrence, retired pilot, captain of the Seaway and later ship inspector, bought the land and built this home. John Lawrence, whose father was also a captain on the river, still has descendants living on the island today. A number of relatives of the Lawrences are currently involved in the river captain and pilotage professions.

The Fisher Home

Built in the early 1900's, the Fisher home was situated on the St. Lawrence River, one mile west of Aultsville at "Anchor Bay" (named after the ships which used to drop anchor in the bay), on one hundred sixty-eight acres. The lot, now underwater, was located south of the present day Crysler's monument east of Morrisburg.

In 1949, Mae and Floyd Fisher bought the home from the Van Allen family and spent a few years in their new community, raising their young children. Among a number of fond memories, the children remember, vividly, the chicken farm activities and the loading of the chickens on the Grand Trunk train to Montreal.

This home is a happy blend of the neo-Georgian and Italianate styles. It has Georgian characteristics such as its two storeys, good proportions, even number of shuttered bays on each side of a front entrance, low hipped roof, and end chimney. Italianate features, such as squareness of the structure, projecting veranda, and low pitched roof are also predominant. At one time, the home was painted red and had a closed-in front veranda, popular at the turn of the twentieth century and later.

During the late 1970's, faithful to the tradition of the embellishment of an already stylish home, the new owners undertook a number of tastefully done renovations which would continue to breathe life into the old structure. In addition to preserving the traditional architectural interior features, enlarging and making a more functional kitchen, the owners added an imposing, circular, double storey front veranda, often preferred by people of better financial means of the late eighteen hundreds. The new handsome columns and the restored front entrance recount this home's historic past.

In 1958, before the flood which would cover the entire property and along with other homes from the same area of the St. Lawrence River, the home was moved five miles (8 km) to the west end of Riverside Heights. The Fisher family recalls with interest the moving day, in 1957, at the crossroads from the river and the old Highway #2. Under the guidance of the traffic police, the home met with Christ Church from Moulinette, also on the way to its new site, in the Upper Canada Village Museum, and was required to detour.

The Fisher farm land situated on the St. Lawrence River was also expropriated to make way for the St. Lawrence project and was used, in part, for the building of Upper Canada Village Museum and the Crysler's Memorial.

The present owners continue to enjoy their recently acquired home and continue to preserve its precious heritage.

The Loucks Home

The Loucks home is a fine example of the prosperity achieved by many loyalist families who settled the land granted to them more than two hundred years ago along the St. Lawrence River. The home was situated on Lot 22, front concession of Williamsburg township, south of old Highway #2, between the banks of the St-Lawrence River and the old River Road, nearly two miles (3.2 km) east of Morrisburg, and west of Aultsville.

It was built on land granted to William Loucks Sr., a United Empire Loyalist who fled the Mohawk Valley, in 1784. William Sr. who had been granted four hundred acres of land had settled in the Aultsville area. Generations of the Loucks family members lived on the property from the time that William Loucks acquired it as a Crown land grant, in 1803, to the construction of the Seaway project.

It is probable that William Loucks, son of Richard Loucks, 1774-1841, a tavern keeper in west Osnabruck, built a one-room shanty for the first year or so. It was, then, followed by a series of larger log or wood frame homes. It was, however, probably his son, John Loucks, a veteran of the Battle of Crysler's farm in 1813, who built the fine stone dwelling. It was a daughter of John Loucks, Catherine, who married Samuel Ault, son of the Loyalist Nicholas Ault, for whom the village of Aultsville was named.

The stone structure home, including the kitchen and a chimney on the opposite side of the main structure, was built sometime in the early 1850s. Of Regency style, its elliptical transom above the front door, flanked by two side windows, adds to its air of elegance and family prosperity.

The Loucks family history reports that descendants bearing the name Laux, Loux, Lauck, Laucks, or Loucks have one common ancestor, the father of Philip and Nicholas Laux, Guillaume Sanche du Laux. Of Palatinate origins, the Laux, along with thirty thousand compatriotes fled to London, England, to escape the horrors of the religious wars raging in the seventeenth century in Europe.

In December 1709, four thousand German Protestants sailed from England on ten vessels and arrived in New York, in 1710. After a few years in the region of the Schoharie Valley, they settled in the Mohawk Valley, where many family members became prosperous. Many of them served in the War of Independence and, as United Empire Loyalists, also served in the War of 1812 between Britain and the United States.

Today, the home stands at the Upper Canada Village Museum on land originally granted to the Loyalist Hickey family. Indeed, the home was moved from the waterfront to Upper Canada Village Museum before the Seaway construction and restored to the 1860's period. The home was picked up in one piece and brought to its present site in the Village, one of the heaviest houses to be moved intact. It reflects a more prosperous period in the life of the riverside communities one decade prior to Confederation in 1867.

It houses many artifacts of the mid-nineteenth century including manufactured furnishings, embroidered decorations, a sewing machine, and kerosene lamps. The Loucks' farm activities included raising chickens, pigs, and cattle as well as the production of dairy products. As farm families did, the Loucks family also bought at the general store imported supplies such as tea, coffee, and molasses to supplement the maple syrup.

Considering that the original settlers strived at making their home self-sufficient, the Loucks home, thus, portrays the prosperity which many loyalist families had reached two or three generations after the original settlers.

The Cook Home

In the early years of settlement, home owners often took out an inn licence as a means to charge their guests. Contrary to the early nineteenth century custom of taking in overnight travelers, the Cook home was built in 1822 to serve as an inn, tavern, and hotel. It was a home away from home for river travelers needing food and a night's rest, either on their way to Montreal from Kingston or on their return trip. Land travelers needed a stopover to rest and/or change horses for overnight travels.

It is reported that sometimes there were up to two hundred guests staying at the inn at one time. As beds were limited, most often travelers slept on straw mattresses on the floor in the largest room of the home. In addition to river and coach travelers, some of the inn guests were lumbermen, priests, bishops, merchants, and lawyers. Other well known inns in the area were the Snyder's at Dickinson's Landing, the Loucks' near the western end of Osnabruck, and the Myers' Inn, east of Morrisburg.

Although some inns, at times, offered poor service, were overcrowded, served bad food, and had uncomfortable beds, the taverns of the early community were the centre of social and community life. They were places to pick up mail, share news, and engage in business deals. The larger room, known as the ballroom, served numerous purposes. It was used mostly for political gatherings, court of law, meeting places, and served as auction centers as well as funeral parlors.

A Loyalist descendant of German origin (family name was originally Van Keugh), Michael Cook took out an inn licence, in 1804. During the battle at Crysler's farm, in early November 1813, General Wilkinson and his defeated American invading army used it as command headquarters and occupied the home for a number of days. This home was burned by the defeated American army. At the end of the war, Cook received government compensatory fund for his losses of farm equipment and family possessions.

It is the inn, built in 1822, by Michael Cook, which now stands at the Upper Canada Village Museum.

History credits Michael Cook's grand-son, Michael Urias Cook, as the one who introduced the Holstein-Friesian cattle breed to Canada in 1881. The home, now known as the Doctor's House at Upper Canada Village, was the home of Michael Urias Cook who built it near the village of Aultsville. The Durham and the Ayshire cattle names were most common prior to that time. A plaque commemorating his contribution to the industry stands on the road to the entrance of the Upper Canada Migratory Bird Sanctuary, west of Ingleside along the County Road #2. Signed by the Ontario Heritage Foundation, an agency of the Government of Ontario, the plaque reads: "In 1881, Michael Cook who operated a prosperous 200 acre farm here imported the first Holstein-Friesian cattle in Ontario. This was part of a movement among progressive farmers to find a breed of cattle that would produce enough milk for Ontario's growing industry, especially cheese production.... The Holstein quickly established its reputation with Ontario farmers and, in 1886, the dairymen's association of Eastern Ontario recognized the Holstein as the leading milk producing breed."

At one time, known as the Garlow (Garlough) house, Cook's tavern faced the river front in the Williamsburg Township, east of Morrisburg and west of Aultsville on Cook's Point. Archival photos reveal that a gable roof dwelling and a mansard roof barn were attached to the inn at the rear. Only the home/inn/tavern was moved to Upper Canada Village Museum prior to 1958. This imposing Loyalist style structure provides insight into the amenities and comforts for the early travelers.

Considering that the mortar did not stand the move, the home was rebricked after the move, taking care to place the better side of the original bricks on the outside. The home was refurbished to its present day graceful status.

The Crysler Home and Evergreen Hall

The Crysler property was situated along the river, south and west of the present day Crysler Memorial Park complex. This historic home is a tangible symbol of the battle at Crysler's farm in 1813. On June 18, 1812, the United Stated declared war against British territories to the north. Although a number of attempts were made to invade Canada, from the west through the Great Lakes, the American's efforts proved futile. Their overall plan was to descend the river towards Montreal, to join land troops east of the rapids, and, together, take Montreal. Cutting off the supply route on the St. Lawrence River became their strategy. Kingston, and then Montreal, were identified as targets.

In the attempts to execute the plan, difficulties ranged from bad weather, bad roads, lack of food and water, and a hostile population. General Wilkinson was put in charge of the American army of nine thousand men while Colonel Joseph Morrison took over the command of the British troops, a mere eight hundred artillery men and cavalry along with local militia from the area.

The American flotilla started on November 6 on its way to what was believed to be a sure victory. Soldiers burned homes and ransacked barns along the way. Fearing that the British forces might attack from the back while the army moved towards Cornwall, the American General decided to tie up at Cook's Point while the officers lodged at Cook's tavern, nine miles west of the rapids. On November 10th , the British forces moved into the area ready to fight the enemy. On November 11, General Wilkinson ordered his men on shore to march towards Cornwall. Lines were drawn up for the battle which would pit the American and the British forces on a cleared field on the farm of John Crysler. Morrison arranged his men in the best manner possible, one group along the St. Lawrence River and the other next to a swamp. The reluctance to cross the gully by the American men, and the charges with bayonets by the Canadians, caused the foe to retreat.

At the end of the battle, forty Americans had been wounded while one hundred had been killed. The British lost twenty-two men, had one hundred forty-seven wounded, and twelve went missing. It is said that the battle at Crysler's farm, on November 13, 1813, saved Canada for Great Britain. Indeed, the battle put an end to the American dream of capturing Montreal.

In 1893, the Canadian government erected a monument on the site of the battle to commemorate the importance of this event in our history. In the 1950s, it became obvious that not only would the monument have to be rescued from the flooded area but most of the battlefield would be lost under the rising waters of the St. Lawrence River. The need to preserve this historic moment led to the creation of the Crysler Memorial Park Centre, east of Morrisburg. It houses the memorial obelisk on a ceremonial mound of soil scooped up from the original battlefield along with an interpretive and display building.

Along with the obelisk, the home of Colonel John Pliny Crysler (1801-1881), built in 1846, was relocated to Upper Canada Village Museum nearby. Often referred to as "Evergreen Hall", its history has been closely associated with the history of the St. Lawrence River and with the famous battle.

The neo-classic style of architecture is featured in the Crysler residence. Moreover, it is of the temple-with-wings form of construction, quite unique in Upper Canada. Its definite size, balance between the horizontal and vertical areas, recessed classical portico flanked by Doric columns, ellipse-shape gable window over the central bays, and double chimneys give it its Classic Revival style.

In 1958, the home was dismantled brick by brick and re-erected on the grounds of Upper Canada Village Museum. Rather than restore its interior, it was decided to reconstruct the residence as a museum with some partitions removed for exhibit space and curatorial offices. A small stone kitchen, on the back of the original home, was detached and restored as a separate home nearby, which, today, is the home of the Village dress-maker.

The Van Allen Home and Cottage

The county of Dundas is composed of Morrisburg, being the largest town, the townships of Williamsburg, Matilda, Winchester, and Mountain. At the conclusion of the War of Independence, disbanded soldiers began farming in this area. Some cut timber for the emerging Montreal markets while others became teamsters, towing boats up the river and moving passengers, as well as goods, between Cornwall and Prescott. Moreover, Morrisburg's geographic location, along the river, at the east end of the canal Rapids Plat locks, south of the townships of Williamsburg and Matilda, and north to Ottawa, has made it the most important village in Dundas county.

This frame house, owned by the Van Allen family, used to be set on Lot 12 of concession one, in Williamsburg Township. Based on its foundation, it can be presumed that the original home, built by the Bush family, was a log dwelling similar to others in the area. It was located on the south side of the King's Highway #2, just east of the junction of the farm lane and the old highway. The farm lot contained many buildings which dated back to the period of the battle at Crysler's farm. It is thought to be the only surviving building from the famous battle. Moreover, since the battle caused a number of casualties, it is presumed that the home was used as a makeshift hospital for the wounded on November 13th. 1813.

In 1784, Loyalist Jacob Van Allen, a lieutenant of General Johnson, had come forcibly to Canada from New York. His two sons, Henry and Gilbert, fought for the Militia against the American invaders at the Battle of Crysler's farm and again at the battle of Windmill Point. Henry's son, Abraham, bought Crysler's farm, about 1870, which until then had briefly been owned by the Bush's, the Jonas', the Croil's, then the Doran's. The Van Allens' called the home the "cottage", as distinct from the main house just north of the King's Highway #2 which was destroyed during the Seaway project. It was used to house the hired man's family. Crysler's farm and its cottage, have been owned by the Van Allen family since 1870. In the 1920s, the "cottage" was operated as a tea room by Mary M. Van Allen, catering to visitors to the nearby monument. In 1958, Mary M. and Blanche Van Allen saved it from destruction by moving it, at their expense, to the nearby riverside village of Morrisburg.

John Pliny Crysler was the son of John Crysler, of Williamsburg and Finch, and of Nancy Loucks. Both were United Empire Loyalists. John Crysler came to this country in 1784, a drummer boy, at the age of fifteen. As a farmer, merchant, and a colonel of the militia, he became financially successful and owned sixty thousand acres of land in the county. In 1850, John Crysler died in Finch at the age of 81. John Pliny became a captain in the Dundas militia and served at the battle of Windmill Point east of Prescott. Before his appointment as the Dundas County Registrar in 1867, he had developed a prosperous mercantile and lumber business.

The Battle at Crysler's farm was one of a number of attacks made by the United States on Canadian British soil. The victory of the British forces ensured the continuity of Canada as a separate entity and as a nation. An obelisk, commemorating the significance of this battle in our Canadian history, was erected in 1893 by the government on the Van Allen farm property donated for that purpose. The monument is a national memorial honouring the British and Colonial troops who fought so bravely at the Battle of Crysler's farm. In 1958, the obelisk was moved to the new County Road #2, about seven miles (11 km) east of Morrisburg and at some distance from the site of the battle.

More than two hundred years ago, in Dundela, in the Township of Matilda, a famous apple was developed. John McIntosh, a United Empire Loyalist from Schenectady, New York, arrived with other Loyalists in 1784. In 1808 he married Hannah Doran. While clearing a bush near his farm, John discovered about twenty apple sprouts, a rare luxury at the time. With the help of a knowledgeable migrant worker, in 1835, he began grafting the trees to produce what we know today as the "MacIntosh Red", known world-wide. Other varieties, which were developed later, are the Melbas and the Lobos.

The finely maintained home, with its medium pitched roof and balanced facade, is an adaptation of the Georgian style. Today, it stands at the west end of Morrisburg along the old Highway #2.

The Farlinger Home

Prior to the construction of the canals, Morrisburg and West Williamsburg were farming communities. The farms fronted the river in long narrow strips. Some of the homes built by the early Loyalist settlers were the Roses (Rosedale), the Farlingers (Belmont), the McKenzie, the Cooks, the Weegans, and the Merkleys. The earliest settlements were along Lock street and east of River Drive.

With the coming of the Grand Trunk Railway, the construction of the canals and the increased trade, more mercantile shops transformed Morrisburg into a centre of commerce for Dundas. There was rapid growth during those years. In 1869, the population was eighteen hundred. By 1878, the population reached two thousand, a close rival of Cornwall. The town was a port of entry and had a customs office. A number of industries flourished. As two of the most significant industries, dairy and poultry products were shipped to all areas of the country.

In the late 1870s, Morrisburg's prosperity was reflected in a number of industrial and commercial blocks, built on Main Street, and named after their owner-merchants. Along the Morrisburg waterfront, there were the Farlinger's block housing the Molson's Bank, the Gibson's Mill and Elevator, the Lyle's Block, the Meikle's, and the Bradfield's Blocks. Many other businesses were shippers, bankers, hotel keepers, tailors, jewelers and a druggist. They were owned by the Broders, the Dardis, the McMartins, the Casselmans, the Gibsons, the Chalmers, and the Carmans.

Morrisburg's flourishing economy was also reflected in its homes. Built by William Kyle, in 1834, and remodelled in 1879, the Farlinger home was situated at the eastern entrance to Morrisburg. This stately and impressive old home was also called the "Belmont" home. The clapboard-siding, twenty-two room home had a number of bays extending outward, and three vertically arranged front balconies, or verandas. Treillage with elaborate patterns at the upper corners of porches and verandas was typical of eastern Ontario from 1835 to 1860. It is sometimes referred to as Victorian or Gingerbread trim. In the Farlinger home treillage extended to all three verandas. Moreover, this home, like other homes in the area, had patterns of fish-scale shingles arranged in various ways.

Family records show that the first Farlinger arrived in British North America in 1710, and settled in Schoharie, New York. One of his descendants, John Farlinger, moved to Upper Canada in 1776, with his wife, Sophia Desrosiers, of French Huguenot descent, and his family. Their youngest child, Nicholas, born in 1768, married a Cornwall girl, and sometime later moved his family to Dundee, Quebec. Alexander Farlinger, grandson of Nicholas, son of James Robert Farlinger and Barbara Gardiner, was born on June 1, 1824.

At the age of nineteen, Alexander left home, and shortly afterwards was put in command of one of the Royal Mail steamers running between Montreal and Kingston. He became captain of the "Lord Elgin" steamship. Following a few successful years, he embarked in a mercantile and shipping business in Prescott. In 1854, he married William Kyle's daughter and settled with his wife's family in Morrisburg. Captain Alexander Farlinger devoted his time to real estate and became very successful. As owner of nineteen thousand acres of land in the Eastern Counties, Alexander Farlinger also owned and operated the Farlinger Block in the business section of Morrisburg.

Between the years 1940 and 1950, a shortage of labour in the Counties, coupled with the uncertainties in Europe, brought a new wave of immigrants to the area - the Dutch. Dutch families lived with sponsors for a year before they bought their own land and slowly began building their herds. It is reported that in 1948, twenty-nine families and twelve single men settled in the area. Like many generous pioneering families, the Farlingers welcomed and mentored Dutch families.

Isabelle Kyle-Farlinger, grand-daughter of William Kyle, and daughter of Alexander Farlinger, was living in the home at the time of the Seaway. Born in 1866, she was ninety-one years old when she moved out to allow Ontario Hydro to destroy the impressive family homestead.

The Rose Home

The Rose home, built by Alexander Rose, was the home of the Rose family. It was situated east of Morrisburg, on land later flooded to make way for the Seaway project. Isaac Newton, son of Alexander Rose, was born on July 14, 1811 on the family homestead. In his youth, Isaac learned the tanner's trade and was one of the first residents to develop the mercantile trade. Large quantities of cordwood, supplied by farmers for steamboat fuel, were retailed from the wharf of I. N. Rose.

On December 13, 1849, Isaac Newton Rose married Ruth Doran. He managed, with integrity and great flair, the extensive farm left to him by his father. It is said that in 1863, Isaac Newton sold land north of the farm to the Board of Trustees of Morrisburg for the erection of two schools in Morrisburg. Again, his sense of justice and leadership was recognized when he was appointed Justice of the Peace. After the village of Morrisburg was incorporated in 1860, Isaac Newton Rose was one of the council members present at its first meeting held in 1861. He later became Reeve of Williamsburg for several years before taking on the duties of Superintendent of the Williamsburg canals. When he died on September 12, 1874, he was greatly missed by many who had fond memories of the gentleman.

The Rose home, facing the St. Lawrence River, was a graceful stone residence, flanked by a log lodge, a number of cottages, and a nine-hole golf course across the old Highway #2, at the rear of the home. In the early 1930s, Ralph Fetterly, a car dealer, and his wife, who owned the home, transformed it into an inn and tourist home, and named it "The Rosedale". As the home was situated along the old Highway #2, and that road was the major route from Montreal to Kingston, the inn flourished. Its red-wine canopy above its majestic entrance welcomed visitors. Its sweeping lawns sloping down to the river provided a relaxing environment. The ten room residence had a side room kitchen above which resided some of the kitchen staff. The large dining room, situated in the screened- in porch, offered a four-mile view of the river with its traveling canallers and steamboats. Rooms were finely appointed and provided a welcome rest for all travellers.

The Hill family bought the Rosedale Inn, in 1948, from Pearl Beaver-Fetterly, and continued to operate it until October 1957, when the Seaway project sealed its fate. As the inn was too heavy to relocate, it was purchased by Ontario Hydro and destroyed. Doris Hill, whose husband had died in 1949, and who had operated the inn singlehandedly, decided to retire following the closure of the inn. The log lodge was purchased and moved to Ault Island by Parker Locke, son of renowned Dr. Locke, and used as a cottage for a few years before its destruction.

Some wall stones were saved and used to build the wall of the Memorial Cemetery at the Upper Canada Village Museum. The others were used to build the fence around the Trinity Anglican Church moved to Riverside Heights in 1957. Originally built in 1835, in the area known as "The Churches" east of Morrisburg, the church had been rebuilt at the turn of the century by Eldwin C. Whitney and his wife, Sarah Crysler, in memory of their parents. The Gothic style church, often referred to as the "Trinity Memorial" and the "Whitney Memorial Church", was taken down stone by stone during the construction of the Seaway project and rebuilt on its present site, along the new County Road #2, in the Riverside Heights community.

In the family plot, at the back of the cemetery, a monument erected in memory of Sir James Pliny Whitney, marks his resting place. Sir James had spent his early childhood west of Aultsville. He attended Cornwall Grammar School and was called to the Bar in 1876. In 1866, he served in the Militia as Lieutenant Colonel during the Fenian Raids. In 1888, he became Leader of the Opposition in the Ontario Legislature and was appointed to the Queen's Council in 1890. After founding the Ontario Hydro Electric Commission, in 1906, he was knighted, in 1908, before his death in New York city, in September 1914.

It is, therefore, fitting that the Rosedale Inn survives, in part, in the fence of the Trinity Whitney Memorial Church as Sir James Pliny Whitney had been instrumental in supporting a better canal system.

The Allison Home

Prior to the Seaway project, the river narrowed on either side of Morrisburg to approximately three-quarters of a mile wide. The three mile long Rapids Plat canal, built in the 1850s', stretched west of Morrisburg to end at Flagg Creek. As the rapids flowed at about seven miles an hour (12 km), the steamers could not ascend the river at that point.

On either side of the boundary line of the international section of the river, there were a number of Canadian and American owned islands. From east to west and fronting Morrisburg, there were Rose's Island and Doran's Island, later re-named Broder Park and Canada Island, in Canada. Dry Island, also known as Corrigan's Island, along with Ogden's, McKean's, and Murphy's islands, were in the United States. They ranged from several hundred acres to a mere twenty-five acres.

Life, on the islands, was a mixture of agricultural activities and summer enjoyment of the river in the form of fishing, boating, and swimming.

The Allison home was situated on Murphy's Island, also named Monck's, Wallbridge's, and Dunn's Island, after their previous owners. Murphy's Island enjoyed high land elevation stretching for one hundred fifty acres, south east of Morrisburg. Originally owned by ship Captain W. Murphy, the island was sold to J.Wesley Allison, in 1899.

Born in the Township of Williamsburg, on May 4, 1862, J.Wesley was the son of David Allison. In 1882, J.Wesley left home and started a successful career as a business and finance executive in New York. His fortunes allowed him to return to his country of birth and purchase the property. The home was a clapboard siding three-storey Queen Anne style home with a wrap-around veranda, multiple balconies, and a tower. The home was described as spacious, charming, and finely appointed.

J.Wesley later refurbished and transformed the old residence into a summer resort and added a number of buildings to the complex. There was a maid service home, a two-storey gable roof boathouse for family and visitors, a boat dock, tennis courts, hardwood-floor horse stables with stained glass windows, and a cattle barn.

Mr. Allison farmed successfully on the island. The family owned cattle, imported sheep, and horses. J. Wesley, who transformed the complex into a tourist resort, also owned and operated a ferry to the island for forty years.

It is reported that in 1911, Mr. J.Wesley Allison opposed an earlier plan for a Seaway project, elaborated in the early 1900s, in a letter he sent to the Right Honorable Wilfrid Laurier. Reasons for his objections to the Government proposed plan were four fold: Canadian approval was ignored, the dams and power houses might be situated in the United States, the plan contravened the Ashbury Treaty requiring unrestricted water access, and no obligation to deliver power to the Canadian shore was required.

It is reported that although some buildings were probably abandoned in the late 1930s, in the early 1950s, following the death of J.Wesley Allison and the uncertainties of the Seaway and Power project, the home was left vacant. In 1958, on July 1st when the water began to rise the home and buildings already had intentionally been destroyed by fire the previous winter as part of the process of clearing land. Allison Island fell prey to the rising waters and reappeared as two separate small islands now facing the east end of Morrisburg.

At the time of the Seaway project, a second Allison family, distant relative of J. Wesley operated a well appointed tourist resort more than one mile (2 km) east of Morrisburg. This property was also razed to accommodate the Seaway project.

The Broder Home

The Broder home is situated on the north side of the Kings's Highway, in Morrisburg. The twenty-two room brick residence was built by William Broder, a village merchant, in 1879. With its mansard roof, projecting tower, decorative iron cresting on the roof, long rounded windows with heavy bracketed eaves, and its vertical irregular outline, the home is a fine example of the Second Empire architecture style prevalent between the years 1860 and 1880.

Andrew Broder, son of William Broder, was born of Irish parents, in Franklin Center, County of Huntingdon, Quebec, on April 18, 1844. In his late thirties, Andrew married Caroline Summers on March 11, 1884, and raised his young family of four children - Harry, Carrie, Willie and Fred - in Morrisburg. In 1875, his political interests and skills led him to be elected Member of Parliament for Dundas, which he held until 1886. His beloved wife Caroline died at childbirth on May 4, 1895. At his death on January 4, 1918, the Honorable Andrew Broder was a Member of the Privy Council. As Doran's Island had reverted back to the Government at the end of its lease, it was renamed Canada Island, and in honor of Andrew Broder the park was named Broder Park.

The Broder home was later sold to J. Wesley Allison, of Allison Island. While J. Wesley and his family lived at the Allison home in the summer, the Broder home was their winter residence. The next owners, Mabel and Ben Carr, transformed the large home into a "Bed and Breakfast" and named it the "Ship's Mate".

The name, reminiscent of another Carr family home, situated along the old canal, called the "Sign of the Ships", was known to attract tourists in the area. It was a frame home built by the ancestors of George Merkley, in 1810. This Merkley home, along with a number of cottages by the canal, had to be expropriated during the Seaway construction. A small lot, a remnant of the original property, a small cottage, the original old well, and the moved home, survived. The home was relocated from the south side to the north end of its original lot, along the King's Highway, in Morrisburg, while the other cottages were destroyed.

While the depression was creating disastrous effects in Canada, Morrisburg, and its surrounding area, experienced an economic boom. Indeed, in the 1920s and 1930s, Dr. Locke had singlehandedly developed the tourist trade in the village and its region.

Dr. Mahlon W. Locke, born in Brinston, Ontario, on February 14, 1880, attended Iroquois and Kempville schools. Following his graduation from Queen's University, in 1905, and post-graduate work in Edinburgh and Glasgow Universities, Dr. Locke settled in Williamsburg.

In 1908, he began his practice, as a country doctor, in his one-hundred acre farm home. Shortly afterwards, his skill in foot manipulation to relieve and cure rheumatic pains, gained him world-wide fame. As his reputation grew, so did the number of patients knocking at his door. It is reported that, in 1928, he was treating two hundred patients a day. Figures as high as one thousand patients a day, in 1932, appear in local archives. Moreover, his work helped to revolutionize the corrective shoe industry.

This enormous influx of patients brought prosperity to Morrisburg, and up and down the river, for miles. Numerous homes, such as the "Sign of the Ship" and the "Ship's Mate" (Broder Home), were converted into tourist homes. When Dr. Locke died in his car on a snow covered road on February 17, 1942, with him partly ended a prosperous economic wave for Morrisburg.

The Broder home, owned by the Carr family in 1958, was later made into a number of apartments showcasing preserved historic features and artifacts of the original Broder home and those of later owners.

The Chamberlain Home

In the late 1870s, Morrisburg's prosperity was reflected in a number of enterprises developed to support the thriving community. Some of them were the shoe stores, millinery shops, general stores, tailor shops, tin shop, undertaking offices, and hardware stores. There were also the law offices of John Pliny Whitney, the offices of Doctors Chamberlain, Sherman, Hickey, and Smith. In 1878, a Music Hall was erected in the Merkley Block. Built by Albert Merkley and his father, H. G. Merkley, the hall opened its doors in 1879 with the Gilbert and Sullivan's "H.M.S. Pinafore". It continued to be an art centre for the community until its destruction to make way for the new shores of the St. Lawrence River.

It is reported that, in 1858, Morrisburg was a thriving village with a population of 600. Indeed, its history tells of many successful enterprises which resulted in the development of numerous historic, unique, and graceful residences.

The Chamberlain home, and a large section of the property with the ancillary buildings, which were expropriated in 1957, is a good example of Morrisburg historic prosperity. The stately Victorian residence, which was spared, was the home of Dr. Thomas F. Chamberlain. It is reported that while on his honeymoon vacation in Atlantic City, he noticed a home similar to one only seen in his dreams. In 1874, he built the three-storey Victorian residence on the old Highway #2, or at the time also known as King's Highway.

Born at Harlem, Ontario, in 1838, Thomas F. Chamberlain, earned his M.D. Degree from Queen's University in 1862. Dr. Chamberlain performed a number of surgeries in the upper part of the home, which he used as a private hospital, indeed, the first hospital in Morrisburg. His talents as an orator led him to be elected a Conservative Member of Parliament shortly after the Confederation in 1857. He served as warden and as an associate coroner of the Eastern Ontario Counties. In 1889, Dr. Chamberlain was appointed Inspector of Ontario Asylums and Prisons. He died in 1927.

The home was sold to Dr. Chamberlains's son, W. P. Chamberlain, then to Albert G. F. Drew and to Watson Parrish. In 1915, Fred H. Meikle purchased the property and sold the Chamberlain home to Michael J. Casselman, father of A. C. Casselman, former M. P., while he retained the river portion of the property to build a home for his family.

The Cardinal family operated the attractive home as a tourist home, known as "The Cardinal", during the days of Dr. Locke's foot clinic. Dr. George M. Gorrell, a dental surgeon, purchased the home in 1939. For many years, his patients used the large entrance as the waiting room, and, to the right, the dining room as the clinic area. In 1954, George William Gorrell, Dr. George's son, purchased the home and undertook a number of restorations to preserve its historic heritage.

During the Seaway, the Meikle home, which was located south of the Chamberlain home, and other buildings were demolished. The land was expropriated and the Chamberlain home, which survived, gained a new waterfront.

The twenty-seven room home contains a library and a solarium/conservatory decorated with eighteen brightly colored stained glass windows in the west wing on the main floor. The ground floor has two floor-to-ceiling fireplaces in the dining room and in the living room, decorated with Shakespearian-inspired motif Italian tiles. Moreover the plaster work around the ceilings is extremely delicate, decorative, and eye-catching. The entrance foyer features a large staircase leading to a number of apartments upstairs. The hardwood floors and the wood trim throughout the home have been carefully preserved. The windows, of which eighteen are on the front facade, are a predominant feature of the home. The intricate woodwork of the porches highlights the craftmanship of those early pioneers.

The present owners take great pride and enjoyment in living in their home and continually strive to maintain its integrity while enjoying all the comforts of home.

The Carman Home and Museum

The Carman name has its origins in the small German settlement of Kehl, in 1524. Family archives show that the name Kehl also appears as Kurmann, Kirmann, Kermann, Kermer and Kirman. It was Michael Carman III, born in 1769, who settled these areas in the late 18th century. He was the son of Michael II, born in 1743, and grand-son of Michael I, born on November 27, 1708, both in the village of Kehl, Germany. The story is told that sometime in 1750, Michael I, with his wife, Magdalena, and young family, traveled through England and were found, eleven months later, resettled in Pennsylvania, in the United States. In the 1760s, Michael Kirmann I and his family moved to New York, to the Mohawk River Valley and prospered. In 1781, the rebels, who confiscated his property, forced Michael's family to move to Canada.

He proceeded to Matilda Township, in 1784, where he took possession of Lot 24, and later of Lot 25, concession one. Starting in 1799, entries in the Williamsburg registry for the name Kermann appear as Carman. Thus, in 1807, Michael Carman III received, by Order-in-Council, five hundred acres of land in Point Iroquois. It can thus be said that most of the old village of Iroquois was settled on land granted to Michael Carman, a United Empire Loyalist, and his descendants.

In 1810, Michael was made captain of one of the companies of Dundas County Militia. It is not clear what role the Carman family might have played in the war of 1812.

Only four homes from Old Iroquois, were not moved during the Seaway project. However, the land surrounding the homes was expropriated. Those homes had been built on higher ground at the east end of the village by various members of the Carman family.

One of these homes, the first one built by Michael Carman circa 1810, was situated on the highest section of Carman land away from the river. It was spared, with the intention of transforming it into a museum. Indeed, the village of Old Iroquois grew between this Carman home and the St. Lawrence River. It was built with quarried stones and white limestone which became common features of the old village. Indeed, a number of similar homes built at the beginning of the nineteenth century caused Iroquois to be dubbed the "Limestone village".

At the time of the Seaway, no descendants of these founders of Iroquois lived in the home. In 1960, the village took over the restoration of the home and completed it for its centennial year in 1967. Today, the home is used as the Carman House Museum. In addition to numerous restoration efforts guided by Peter J. Stokes, restoration architect, the roof has been re-shingled with cedar shingles. It still has a stone sink in the kitchen, a bake oven for bread making, and two large stone fireplaces.

During the summer tourist season, guides provide tours and information. On its walls are scenes of Iroquois and portraits of pioneers of the early village. A collection of memorabilia of an Iroquois hero, Lt. Col. Lorne Winfield Mulloy, are also displayed. Mulloy, a 20 year volunteer veteran with the British forces in South Africa, was blinded during the Boer War. He went on to graduate with a law degree and to teach military history and strategy at the Royal Military College in Kingston. He returned to Iroquois and continued his law practice until his death, in 1932.

Michael's sons each had a stone home, one of which, still standing and thought to be built by a Carman family member, today is the home of the Iroquois Lawn Bowling Club.

A third Carman home, situated on Elizabeth Drive, was a large colonial-type, two-storey frame dwelling, owned by the Dwight Hamilton family. Originally named "Rosemont" because it had a large rose garden, the home was later renamed the "Playfair", by its owners. It was built in 1892 by Ansel B. Carman, local businessman and merchant tailor. In the mid-fifties, Dr. Peter Playfair bought it from Ontario Hydro for his parents, and lived in the home until his death in 1995. The "Playfair" home was demolished in the year 2001 to make way for a more modern family home.

Moreover, to relocate the new Iroquois, two hundred acres of farm land, owned by James Everett, son of Peter P. Everett, were expropriated by Ontario Hydro over a period of five years, 1953 to 1958.

The Carman Home

The Carman home is situated on Elizabeth Drive in New Iroquois. It is a one and a half storey stone farmhouse, built in 1819, by the Carman family, Michael III, his wife, Regina Link of Williamsburg, and his sons Jacob, Mathew, Peter, and Philip. During the construction of the Seaway, the home was saved while the land surrounding the property was expropriated almost entirely. Although it was not moved, the home gained a closer view of the river.

The old village of Iroquois, as it was referred to prior to 1958, was located on the east side of Point Iroquois along the St. Lawrence River, eight miles west of Morrisburg in the Township of Matilda, in the county of Dundas. It was built on a five hundred acre land grant made to Michael Carman III in 1807. Moreover, the point of land reaching out into the St. Lawrence River was approximately five hundred yards (457 m) from the American shores. At one time, Iroquois was named Rockway. Later, it was re-named Cathcart, in honour of Lord Cathcart, a former Commander of the British Army in Canada. In 1857, it was incorporated and the old village was renamed Iroquois, in memory of the Iroquois natives.

Like many villages along the St. Lawrence River, Old Iroquois owed its prosperity to the construction of both the canals and the arrival of the Grand Trunk Railway during the mid-nineteenth century. The Galop canal, seven and one-half mile (12 km) long, designed to avoid the Galop Rapids south east of the Old Iroquois, severed Point Iroquois from the mainland, at its west end. Using the business opportunity afforded by the new canal, the old village slowly expanded. Moreover, the railway, which was situated immediately north of the village, helped support the growing economy.

In 1954, the Old Iroquois village stood in the way of two major elements of the Seaway and Power projects - the control dam and the new deeper canal to be built at Point Iroquois. It had to be relocated north of its former site and all homes, as well as other buildings, had to be moved or destroyed. Thus, Ontario Hydro expropriated three hundred and nineteen acres of land along the river and north.

Originally surrounded by a large farm with a number of outbuildings, this stone dwelling was a short distance from the other Carman homes. On the east side of the home, a seventy-foot (21.3 m) well was dug by hand and lined with a number of courses of stone-work. The home had a cast-iron sink in the large open-concept kitchen. There were three fireplaces with limestone hearths. Flanking the kitchen fireplace were two wall-end cabinets. The living room and parlor were more formal rooms with eight-inch wide floorboards, wide baseboards and trim, hardwood ceiling beams, raw stone work, and massive hearths. Upstairs there were two bedrooms facing the east and one large room on the west side.

In 1907, the home was sold to William Hamilton Martin, from Aultsville. Mr. Martin, his wife Eliza Jane Crobar, and their children Arthur, Jessie, Sadie, and Clifford, lived in the home until it was sold again by Robert W., grandson of William H. Martin, in 1997. Frank and Ypie Buwalda bought the property and restored it to its original historic state, while adding modern amenities. Central heating was installed, all wood trim, floors, ceilings, and old doors were restored. A new, well appointed bathroom was built upstairs in a roof dormer with the half moon loyalist style fan light cut out of the front roof of the home. The two skylights added to the low kitchen ceiling have added much needed daylight. The exterior stones which had been covered by stucco over the years were restored and re-pointed. A front veranda, decorated with subtle gingerbread trim on the central gable, completed the restoration work.

The present owner, who purchased the home a few years ago and who enjoys finely restored antiques, felt at home from the first visit. This Carman home is a living testimony of Ontario's rich historic past. Undoubtedly, the home deserves the recently given name "Elizabeth Manor".

The Williamson Home

Early pioneers who settled along the St. Lawrence River in Iroquois, were the United Empire Loyalists. Some of them were the Carmans, the Krauses, the Coons, the Walters, the Elliots, the Griers, the Aults, and the Brouzes. A small grist mill was built by the Krauses, while it is reported that a first store was opened by the Brouses, in 1804. Many of the early settlers supplied steamers with wood. The Old Iroquois village held its first council under the presidency of George Brouse, Reeve, and Richard Carman, Town Clerk.

From the beginning of its history, the Iroquois Native Americans used Point Iroquois as a stopover during their journeys either north or south. Amid the lush forest, they built camp-fires and held their pow-wows. The entire area was made up of bush land, orchards, and rich fertile farmlands. A few homes dotted the landscape on the north east corner of the Point. The St. Lawrence River shifted south around the point as it flowed eastward and created a bay in front of the village east of the point.

Built by Austin Doran (1822 - 1886), mill owner and operator, the Williamson home was situated on King Street east, fronting the bay, in Old Iroquois. During the 1800s, Austin Doran, who built a number of homes in Iroquois and Morrisburg, had leased an island east of Iroquois from the Canadian Government and used its grounds as summer pasture for his cattle. Today, the island is referred to as Canada Island.

Early owners of the home were Mr. Bell, a lawyer from Toronto, followed by the R.J. and Emma Ellis family. Over the years, a number of renovations had modified the original home into apartments and eventually into a nursing home. Indeed, before the Seaway project started, Mr. and Mrs. Ed. Williamson operated a nursing home, in the residence, for five years in Old Iroquois.

In 1957, the Williamson home was relocated to New Iroquois on Brouse Drive. Since then, the home has been referred to as the "Williamson Home". It was the largest home moved by the James Hartshorne House Moving Company. The movers used three sets of dollies, with eight wheels each to move the home three quarters of a mile (1.2 km). Four days were needed for the move and an additional several weeks were required before the home was ready to received its five former patients. The five patients had been housed at the Cornwall hospital during the transfer.

Chester and Vera Warren purchased the three-storey, fifteen-room home from Ontario Hydro and continued to operate it as a nursing home. In 1973, the home, which had been transformed into a three-apartment dwelling, was sold to Marilyn and Denis Boissonneault who have lived in it ever since. Throughout the years, their restoration efforts have brought the old residence back to life as a single family dwelling. They have uncovered unique wood trim treasures. The large wood staircase with carved railing posts, flanked by two sets of double doors have been stripped to show the skill with which their carpenters had fashioned them. The finely etched and leaded stained glass windows required only light polishing to reveal their absolutely delicate patterns. The cistern, built in the attic, provided gravity-fed kitchen and bathwater. The home was originally heated by coal and had five fireplaces. Although it was later heated with oil and gas, today there is only one elaborate Victorian style fireplace left in the large dining room, while the home is gas and water heated. The ornate brass and marble radiator covers have been returned to their original state. All four bathrooms and the kitchen have been retrofitted with stylish traditional, yet modern, fittings.

Over the years, previous owners and their relatives have returned to tell stories of fond memories of the home. Feelings of warmth within its walls lingered with them. The owners, who continue to enjoy their home, take great pleasure and pride in their efforts. While their restoration work helps preserve our heritage, it also honours the original home builders and pays homage to their expertise and their great building skills.

The McCall-Caldwell Home

The home was built, circa 1930, by Robert McCall, who worked in the administration office at the Caldwell Linen mills, and his wife, Frances Caldwell, daughter of Robert Caldwell. During the Seaway construction the relocation of the McCall-Caldwell home on Bay Avenue, facing the park, required special equipment and many days. Due to its size and its extreme weight, the Hartshorne House Moving Company required special equipment and many days for the transfer. Florence and Charles Hodgert, manager of the Bank of Montreal in Iroquois, moved into the home. Some of the subsequent owners have been Dr. Munroe, the Levesque family, and the Lewis family.

Amongst its unique features, the two storey-and-a-half Georgian style home has a library-reading room, hardwood flooring attic and concrete clapboard. The large entrance way leading to the living room and dining room with their well preserved alcoves, the fireplace used during the 1998 ice storm, the rounded archways, the stippled stuccoed walls and ceilings, the glass doorknobs with original locks and keys, the wide baseboards, and wood trim throughout the home have all been preserved. The maid's quarters, uncommon at the time, are situated apart from the family living area, at the rear of the home on the second floor.

More than any other enterprise, the Caldwell Mills brought a wave of prosperity to Iroquois. In addition to the numerous hotels, mills, and general stores, the Caldwell Mills, owned by Messrs. J. B. Gass and Robert Caldwell, brought much wealth and recognition to the old village of Iroquois. In 1902, Robert Caldwell arrived in Canada, from Ireland, and, in 1906, settled in Iroquois. The first linen mill called the Dundas Linen Mill was situated on concession one, Lot 25, in the Matilda township. As it never realized good profits, a new mill, built in 1923, specializing in the manufacture of towels, grew and continued to expand until the death of Robert Caldwell in 1934. His son, Herbert H. Caldwell took over the company with its two hundred eighty-five employees. The demand for cotton replaced that of linen, during the Second World War. In 1951, Caldwell Linen Mills was taken over by Dominion Textiles, major producer of cotton products.

In 1954, it was estimated that approximately eleven hundred people had to be moved. Two hundred eighty buildings including homes, commercial properties, schools, churches, and municipal offices had to be relocated. In 1954, a graduate of the University of Toronto school of Architecture, H.H. Roberts, assisted the town council of the village as town planner. His proposal featured a residential area reaching to the water front, churches, and schools dispersed throughout so as to serve the community, a reserved waterfront green belt, administration buildings located north west, and reserved room for community expansion.

Considering that a number of families worked at the plant, and that the company owned and rented thirty-three homes in the village, settlement on the location for a new mill was key to the relocation of the new town of Iroquois. The decision was finally reached when Ontario Hydro agreed to rebuild the Caldwell Linen mills within the corporate boundaries of Iroquois.

A third expanded mill was opened in 1957 and manufactured specialty towels of all kinds which were shipped throughout the world. The mill continued to prosper and with changing markets, Caldwell/Dominion Textiles acquired Wabasso product lines. Fieldcrest Cannon Inc. acquired the trade names, in 1993, and continued to diversify the towel industry to rugs, decorative bedding, and sheets of the finest quality.

The Herbert H. Caldwell home, which at one time served as the W.E. Fitzsimmons Funeral Home, was moved to Iroquois on Beach Street.

The present owners who have been in the former McCall-Caldwell home for ten years have enjoyed restoring the home and preserving its history. Former owners of the home, residents of Old Iroquois, and visitors have returned, time and time again, to tell stories of fond memories when the home was a feature of Old Iroquois.

Part Three

« Found Communities »

The Gallagher Home

It was the dawn of a new day after the old villages had been destroyed and the new communities were starting to emerge. The founding of new communities had been labelled by Ontario Hydro as the rehabilitation phase of the Seaway project. It was the beginning of the new era.

Although the scars of land destruction were covered when the water rose to create a new shore, for many residents it was doubtful if the scars of personal loss would ever heal. The story is told by the present owner of the Gallagher home that, as a war bride of Irish origin, she was experiencing a new beginning when she arrived in Mille Roches, in 1942. Indeed, she was looking forward to better times in Canada. The young couple purchased the home which Alf Johnson had sold to Ontario Hydro.

Built by Art Gallagher in Mille Roches circa 1900, the two-storey home was moved to Long Sault during the Seaway project. Following a few renovations, done to meet regulation standards, such as indoor plumbing and electricity, the home also showed scars. Indeed, upper windows cut into the roof are remnants of those modifications undertaken after the relocation. The young family raised three children in the home, and recalls, with fond memories, the many happy years spent under its roof.

Much publicity had surrounded the progress of the construction project from its beginning to the great flood. In 1957, in the heart of the construction period, it is reported that more that thirty-three thousand visitors had been given tours by university students, teachers, medical students, and Ontario Hydro employees to visit and appreciate the magnitude of the project and the outstanding engineering achievement.

The Inundation Edition of the Standard-Freeholder published on Saturday, June 28, 1958, acknowledged the founding contributors of our communities and the profound transformation of the lives of the riverside villagers. The special edition was a celebration of the human and engineering endeavours which the Seaway and Power project had been.

Although trans-Atlantic ships were able to use the Seaway on July 4, 1958, the opening ceremonies and celebrations for the big project spread over the next year. In fact, there were three major celebrations of the Seaway and Power project, one on September 5, 1958 which was held at the Power Dam with provincial, local, and American dignitaries. The second one was held on April 29, 1959 at the Montreal entrance to the Seaway when the coast guard accompanied a number of ships now able to sail to the Great Lakes with ten times the load of the original canallers and boats. The third one, official opening day, was held on June 26, 1959, east of the St. Lambert Locks, in the presence of Her Majesty Queen Elizabeth II, Prince Phillip, and Mr. B.J. Roberts, President of the St. Lawrence Seaway Authority of Canada, who represented Canada. They were accompanied by President Dwight Eisenhower and by Mr. Lewis G. Castle, administrator of the St. Lawrence Seaway Development Corporation, who represented the United States. The Royal Yacht Britannia continued on for a few days and sailed with its dignitaries toward the Great Lakes, stopping in Cornwall and allowing the land tour to visit Long Sault, Ingleside, Morrisburg, and Iroquois for a number of celebrations along the way.

While tourists and visitors had toured the construction sites, it was the dawn of a new day for the new communities' residents. Attempting to provide leadership, the various guest speakers and leaders across the two nations had echoed each other's version of what the future held for the new communities. Their messages acknowledged that although our roots are deep in the land, our fathers' dreams of a great St. Lawrence Seaway and Power project was now a reality. They repeated that communities must look to the future as a source of new opportunities and of a better life. They emphasized that it is up to us to face the challenges brought about by the Seaway project. They invited us to create our new communities, and in the footsteps of our forebears many years ago, find within ourselves the courage to build new relationships and transform our communities into new homes.

The Gallagher home stands as a symbol of our new beginning which we faced with courage, determination and hope.

The Johnston Home and the Eatwell Bed and Breakfast

The rehabilitation of the new communities consisted of the replacement of the villages in the new settlements. Thirty-seven thousand acres of land in Stormont and Dundas counties were purchased and expropriated for that purpose. In addition, the strip villages of Lakeview Heights, near Cornwall, and Riverside Heights, west of Morrisburg, were also entirely built. The newly built 401 Highway supported the expected industrial expansion. Space, in the new villages, had been set aside for hundreds of new homes and offices. Access to the waterfront and promotion of the tourist industry were facilitated by the construction of parks, green areas, and roads alongside the river. If the industrial boom were to materialize, six thousand acres of land between Morrisburg and Ingleside were reserved for expansion.

The Johnston home, "The Eatwell - Better Beds for Less" embodies the three major phases of the implementation of the Seaway and Power project - the destruction, the construction, and the rehabilitation.

The destruction of the old villages started at the hamlet of Maple Grove and in the bustling village of Mille Roches with the diversion of Highway #2 around the work site. The Provincial Paper Mill factory, already vacant, became the headquarters for some of the Ontario Hydro staff. As workers started to pour in from outside the area, a number of homes opened their doors to them.

Twenty-two thousand construction workers flooded the area. Under the supervision of 500 engineers, handling seventy-five million dollars worth of machinery, the landscape started to change radically. A giant coal-digging machine, brought from Kentucky and nicknamed 'The Gentleman', bit into the earth, twenty tons at a time. Bridges, dams, and channels were destroyed, while piles of rock and sand rearranged the landscape.

The Johnston home, "The Eatwell - Better Beds for Less" former hotel and general store in Mille Roches was also the home of the Johnston family. Attached to the general store owned and operated by Estella and Percy Johnston, the Eatwell was the home of the five Johnston family members. The front door of the two-storey home welcomed visitors into a large living room which led into an equally large formal dining room and then on into the winter and summer kitchens at the rear. Steep staircases, front and back, led up to the vast second floor with approximately twenty bedrooms and two baths. The gas pumps in front of the store were known features of the Johnston family business.

Stalks of bananas, horse collars, shoes, bullets, meat, and cheese were but a few of the items displayed in both store windows and sold at the store. It was well known that Percy Johnston owned and enjoyed race horses. Many a Saturday evening was spent with family and friends sitting on the upturned boxes and nail kegs around the store's 'floor furnace', discussing sports and horses (mostly horses) and other important topics of the week.

During the Seaway construction, it continued to be a home for the Johnstons and their youngest daughter. Known to be a home away from home, the former hotel was reborn into a Bed and Breakfast for hungry, hard working Seaway workers. On a regular basis, thirty-two construction workers lived at "The Eatwell", often sleeping up to six in a large bedroom, each with a cot and a small dresser, and making the best of the situation. Having left their families behind for long periods of time, these men delighted in the antics of the eight year old Johnston girl. In turn, she enjoyed the presence of the "extra fathers" with whom to share stories, songs, and small and big childhood achievements.

The Johnston home was too large to be relocated and so, over a period of many months, it was dismantled by family members. The Johnston Home and The Eatwell was used as building material for the rehabilitation of the new cottage community on what became Lot 48, Moulinette island (Island 17). Its happy memories live on.

The Shannette Home

The construction plans for the new communities included the relocation of homes, schools, churches, stores, cemeteries, and other community services as well as historical sites. Two new towns were created to receive the homes from the lost villages. They were Long Sault and Ingleside. Iroquois, as an entire town, was moved further north, while a number of homes and the whole business section of Morrisburg were relocated north east of the town.

The construction plan, which preceded the rehabilitation program, was to ensure that the residents would have much better municipal services and a generally higher standard of amenities. The rehabilitation program for the new communities was to provide for, as quickly as possible, steady development of residential, commercial, industrial, and recreational areas. Water supply, sewage system, and electric power were some of the important features of the new communities. Moreover, it was expected that the population would grow up to twelve thousand residents in some communities.

Miles of sidewalks, roads, ditches with galvanized culverts, street grading, home walkways, driveways, garage slabs, and home foundations were necessary. At one point, it is reported that four hundred feet (122 m) of sidewalk were built daily. Other construction-related tasks were the surveying of land, the laying of gravel, the continuous winter road repairs, and re-grading of damaged roads while homes were being moved. In addition, the construction of churches, schools, community centres, shopping centres, water pumping stations, and sewage treatment plants, as well as a 208,000 gallon (944,320 liters) water tank were some of the other required construction projects.

Some of the construction companies responsible for the laying out of the new communities were from Montreal, Cornwall, and the wider area. The Cruikshank company, founded in 1956 and owned by Les Cruikshank, was largely responsible for road grading and road construction in the new towns. Ingleside, Morrisburg, and Iroquois, as well as the Long Sault Parkway, and a section of the new 401 Highway, were built by the growing company and continue to be maintained by the same company to this day.

The Shanette home, built by Ronald Hummel for Dr. Shannette in 1941, was moved from its riverside location to the back of the new Morrisburg shopping centre at the time of the Seaway project. Dr. Shanette, a general practitioner, sold the home in 1961 and moved to Mariatown. It is with affection that Doctor Shannete is remembered for his assistance with a larger number of births in the Morrisburg area. It was also Doctor Shannete who provided medical assistance to Dr. Locke during a heart attack which took his life in 1942.

After running the enterprise from a trailer park for two years, the family bought the home and raised three children. The Cruikshanks transformed the doctor's waiting room and office into the young company's office, and family den, respectively. Les, who was born in Bristol Township, Québec, had worked on a number of Ontario Hydro projects in Peru, South America, and in the Niagara area.

At the beginning of the Seaway, in 1956, the young man saw an interesting business opportunity. He traded his brand new car for a road grader which he drove back to Morrisburg from Toronto for the purpose of building the new communities. The purchase of a front-end loader, operated by Les's brother, allowed the business to expand and grow. In 1963, the successful company moved to a new location east of Morrisburg along the new #2 Highway. The company which has remained in the area, has continued to expand ever since and to support community projects.

Although the home was sold again in 1973, and has had a few recent renovations, it is relatively unchanged from what it was in 1954.

The Town of Long Sault and the Long Sault Rapids

The town of Long Sault was named in recognition of the Long Sault Rapids which were flooded during the Seaway project. By 1958, they were buried up to seventy feet (21.3 m) deep in the newly created Lake St. Lawrence, thirty-five miles (56 km) long by three miles (4.8 km) wide, west of the Moses-Saunders powerhouse at Cornwall. Along with the old navigation facilities, the canals and locks, the Long Sault Rapids disappeared forever. However, coffer-dams, built in 1957 to divert the water temporarily, allowed a last look at the bedrock as it was laid bare for a number of months.

The name " Long Sault" evokes a number of thoughts and fond memories for the former residents of the lost villages and of the riverside communities. It makes reference to the rapids which, for centuries, slowed the flow of the river around Sheek's and Barnhart islands. Some adventurers even believed that a channel of sufficient depth for navigation existed through the rapids. Occasionally, an audacious resident would shoot the rapids in a canoe. While descending the rapids, steamers would offer vacationers and travellers a thrilling adventure. Moreover, this magnificent bedrock over which the St. Lawrence River flowed, with great turbulence, was a rare sight. As an endless source of inspiration, the rapids were widely admired by artists, photographers, and those who enjoyed its beauty and power.

The name Long Sault is a also a reminder of the French explorers who sailed the river prior to the arrival of the United Empire Loyalists. Indeed, the "l" in Sault, a remnant of the old french language, is undoubtedly a reminder of the fur traders', explorers', and missionaries' presence during the sixteenth and seventeenth centuries.

The task of closing down communities and acquiring new land suitable for their relocation was a monumental undertaking. Other responsibilities were land surveying for new boundary lines, designing new communities, legal search of titles, signing of agreements for homes to be destroyed or moved, laying out of water and sewer services, roads, and sidewalks. Twelve hundred serviced lots within the township were also developed. In addition, dredging of the lake bottom displaced 250,000 cubic yards (19,114 cubic m) of earth used to reshape the shores and to allow small boats access to the land.

The town of Long Sault, built on the Winters-Cline-Welch-Cass-Mullin farms, is situated on the rolling land facing Lake St. Lawrence with its picturesque islands. Indeed, the Long Sault Parkway, a chain of interconnected islands - survivors of the flood - opens its doors at the foot of the village of the same name. Situated seven miles (11.2 km) west of Cornwall, Long Sault received the residents of Moulinette, Mille Roches, and Maple Grove.

The new town received one hundred twenty-eight homes, while a few more homes were moved along the new Highway #2 to Lakeview Heights. Some owners of cottages on Sheek's Island were relocated to Moulinette Island (Island 17) facing the town of Long Sault. The cottages were slid along the ice in the winter to their new destination. Two schools, four churches, a new Police and Fire department, a shopping mall, modern sewage and water facilities, and miles of sidewalks were some features of the new community.

As huge as the engineering and construction projects were, the rehabilitation of all the new communities, including Long Sault, in form and in spirit, called upon the resourcefulness of residents and families. In each new community, a citizen's committee, made up of one or two members from each of the previous villages, had the mandate to identify needs, allow for a name to be found, assist the residents with the smooth transition to their community, and ensure the implementation of the Seaway project.

In 1981, twenty-five years after the completion of the Seaway project, the town of Long Sault announced a population of 1,100 and an ever expanding economy and prosperity. Tourism, recreation, education, safety and security services, health services, and the large number of volunteers who continually support the various organizations in the town have transformed the Long Sault community into a home.

While the rapids of the great St. Lawrence River were flooded and silenced, the river calmed, its channels deepened, and its hydro electrical power tapped, the town of Long Sault, situated some distance from the water, lives on to recall the memory of the rapids.

The Ingleside Home

In 1955, the task of the Osnabruck Township Council was to name New Town #1 created to replace the villages of Aultsville, Farran's Point, Dickinson's Landing, and Wales. Since "Ingleside" was an old name in the area, Reeve Thorold Lane proposed it for the new community. Hoping its meaning "fireside" or "by the hearth" would reflect warmth and friendliness in the new tow, the council adopted the name.

"Ingleside" was the name of the Hickey home, in Williamsburg Township, about one and a half miles (3 km) west of what was to become the village of Aultsville. The home was built by John Hickey, a United Empire Loyalist, on land granted to him for his service in the American Revolution. The original one-and-a-half-storey dwelling was remodelled in 1914-1915, to add another bedroom, a sun-porch, a dining room, and a larger living room.

The property, which had retained its same appearance up to the time of the Seaway project, remained in the Hickey family from 1784 until its purchase and dismantling by Ontario Hydro and used to build a part of the Upper Canada Village Museum. In addition, the village of Aultsville, which was situated nine miles (14 km) east of Morrisburg and twenty miles (32 km) west of Cornwall on the bank of the St. Lawrence River on old Highway #2, was completely destroyed.

Grandsons of John Hickey, Rubin, Charles, and Samuel A. Hickey graduated from McGill University, in 1874, in medicine. Dr. Samuel Alan also had a home in the village of Aultsville where he settled and practiced for sixteen years. His two brothers practiced medicine in the Morrisburg area. In 1893, at the age of 45, Dr. Samuel A. Hickey died while he was resident physician of the Grand Trunk Railway, in Montreal. His Aultsville home was the last building standing after the demolition of the village of Aultsville.

Some of the Hickey homes had been built by the Sampson brothers who were framers, joiners, and cabinet-makers. Indeed, from the mid to the end of the nineteenth century, George and James Sampson built a number of homes in the village and in its surrounding area.

The Hickey homes are a testimony of the Hickey's contribution to their community. Moreover, the Sampson homes are a symbol of the skill and creativity of those early builders of homes which were destroyed during the Hydro project. Their legacy lives on in the new village of Ingleside.

The village of Ingleside was built on two hundred acres of farm land belonging to Almer Pruner, Willard Rutley, Edward Hart, James River, and Frank Campbell, expropriated by Ontario Hydro. With a population of approximately two thousand, it is situated thirteen miles (20 km) west of Cornwall, on the shores of Lake St. Lawrence. From 1954 to 1957 families chose lots for their new or moved homes and began the period of adaptation and community building.

Originally under two school boards, the new school was named Rothwell-Osnabruck after H.D. Rothwell, Hydro engineer, who directed the rehabilitation program between Iroquois and Cornwall. Four churches were built, dotting the four corners of Memorial Square, to replace the former riverside churches. Funds to build the Library were donated by the Women's Institute of Farran's Point, Aultsville, and Wales. Until the Library was built, the late Fran Laflamme, teacher and historian, was instrumental in setting up a lending Library which started in a corner of the first general store. A health clinic, a fire department, sports and recreation activities served by dedicated residents, have contributed to the emergence of Ingleside as a home community.

The Chamber of Commerce, initially created at the completion of the Seaway project, has been revived recently with the goal of exploring ways to better serve the small community which has continued to grow since its creation in 1958.

The Doran Home

The Doran home, built in 1858 by Austin Doran, merchant, gentleman, and businessman, is situated on the original two hundred seventy-five acre land granted to Jacob and Michael Merkley, of the King's Royal Regiment of New York. Austin Doran owned the carding mill, part of the early industrial complex which occupied the east end of River Drive in the old Morrisburg. Austin Doran, who had leased an island south of Morrisburg from the Canadian Government, encouraged the citizens of Morrisburg to enjoy their leisure time on the island, for picnics and over-night camping. Annual picnics were held on this island until the ferry service ended in 1954. Thus, it could be said that Austin Doran was the father of Morrisburg's Parks and Recreation Department.

The home was later sold to Francis B. Maxwell, and again, circa 1907, sold to Reverend W. T. MacKenzie. The Bush family who owned it from 1908 to 1929 sold it to the Crober family. It is reported that at one time, there were cots wall-to-wall upstairs for those children who were billeted in the home on snowbound days.

As the oldest home on the street, it possesses all of its original charm, from the carriage house, wood shed, summer kitchen, and maid's quarters. The home enjoys much of the natural light through its original grand windows. The wrap around veranda shelters the lower windows from the hot summer sun, allowing for low maintenance air-conditioning of the interior. The Wallaces, who acquired the home in 1989, have undertaken extensive restoration to return the home to its original simple charm. They often welcome back former owners of the home and their relatives who share stories of fond memories of their stay.

Although the home was not moved, some 145 years later, as a consequence of the Seaway project and the expropriation of a part of the old village of Morrisburg further north away from the flood waters, the home is now located at the south end of the Village. Furthermore, to facilitate the implementation of the emergency assistance measures in the late 1990s, the street name was changed from Church Street to Sir James Morris Drive.

The growing village, known as West Williamsburg, was named Morrisburg in 1851, in honor of Sir James Morris and was incorporated in 1860. Sir James Morris, a resident of Brockville, was born in Paisley, Scotland, in 1798, and arrived in Upper Canada with his parents in 1801. Amongst his numerous accomplishments is his role as a commissioner for the improvement of navigation on the St. Lawrence River. Indeed, he was instrumental in promoting and financing the construction of the Williamsburg canals. In 1851, when Canada assumed the responsibility for the Royal Mail, Sir James Morris was appointed Canada's First Postmaster General.

In appreciation for the recognition paid him by the people of Morrisburg, Sir James Morris donated one hundred dollars to the Village to assist in the purchase of either a town clock or bell. A bell, in his honor, had been placed over the town hall and remained there for one hundred years. It was moved to the Morrisburg Public School during the Seaway project. In 1992, it was moved again to a newly built clock tower in the centre of the Morrisburg public plaza. James Morris died in Brockville in 1865.

At the beginning of the 1900s, the elegance of its residences and the beauty of its shores were the chief attractions for Morrisburg. In 1958, the Seaway project caused a section of the village to be flooded, thus, reshaping its shores. While some homes were destroyed, eighty-seven homes were relocated to higher ground, within the new town of Morrisburg, on land largely expropriated from the Farlinger's, The Allison's, and the Van Allen's farmlands. Twenty-one homes were moved to Williamsburg Township, while the entire original business district was completely destroyed. A new shopping centre, with modern conveniences, was built, as a unit, north of the original town along the newly redrawn former Highway #2. The old railway bed was used for the laying out of the new County Road #2. The Railway track was moved one mile (1.6 km) north of the new town.

The thriving community of Morrisburg, with its rich and diverse heritage, continues to enjoy prosperity and to expand its vision for the future.

The Tindale Home-Lockmaster's House

The Tindale home, one of the last original homes from Old Iroquois which embodies the spirit and heritage of early pioneers, is now referred to as the Lockmaster's house. The Victorian style home, which overlooks the Iroquois Seaway locks, was the home of lockmasters until 1997. Built circa 1892, the large three-storey frame house, with its easterly tower resembling a light house, was later the home of John Dixon Harkness and his family of nine children. In 1923, James W. Tindale and his wife, Mary Rebecca, bought the home and took up residence with their three daughters. As James W. Tindale was very entrepreneurial, he owned a number of businesses in the village of Iroquois - jewellery, silverware, and insurance. From the store, his daughters operated the first telephone line service.

The dwelling, situated on high ground, was not destroyed during the Seaway project. It was surrounded by an orchard and a number of homes and cottages, one of which was the Pine Grove Resort. In 1954, while Point Iroquois was carved out to make way for the new Seaway canal, the property was expropriated. Today, it is managed by the St. Lawrence Seaway Management Corporation. It stands at the edge of a forty foot (12.2 m) embankment facing the locks. On the north side of the house, the land gradually slopes down to the locks of the Old Galop Canal, built in 1846.

As was with many villages along the St. Lawrence River, the old canals and the arrival of the Grand Trunk Railway were instrumental in bringing prosperity to the village of Iroquois. The lockmaster was hired as a government employee and was provided with a residence for himself and his family. Since his responsibilities included the operation and the maintenance of the locks, carpentry, masonry, and clerk skills were required. Summer and winter, he would regulate the water level and carry on maintenance repairs while the locks were not in use. He was required to keep toll books and a number of other canal records.

During the construction of the Iroquois Seaway lock, the Ontario Hydro staff transformed the home into an operations centre. In 1958, Tom McCaffery, the first Lock Superintendent, moved into the home. In 1964, he was followed by Gordon McDonell who retired in 1984, and then by Jean Paul Bernier, the last Superintendent in this house. Since the introduction of the Seaway Shipping and Power project, the construction of the new electrically-powered lock, and the creation of a new management system, lockmasters are no longer required.

After 1958, the New Village of Iroquois was established on land north of the Old Iroquois, near the old town boundaries. The farmlands of James Everett, Martin, Hamilton, and Brouse were expropriated to accommodate the new village. Ontario Hydro set-up five stopover homes to ease the transition for one's move from the old village to the new site. New homes were built while one hundred fifty others were moved and refurbished between the fall of 1955 and the fall of 1957. Other homes were destroyed by fire or bulldozer. Old homes were scattered among new ones and along streets named after those families who had left their mark in the community. Residents planted trees near their homes and slowly began to settle in their new environment. New municipal offices with fire department and library, shopping plaza, schools, and churches were built to replace the lost ones. Golf, tennis, horse back riding, and lawn bowling were gradually re-established. The New Iroquois waterfront area continues to be popular for fishing, boating, and camping. In tandem with the development, the population has continued to expand to 1,212 citizens in 1997.

In 1999, the Tindale home was destined for destruction. Saved by the recently founded DIAMONDS Land Trust, it has been transformed into the St. Lawrence Seaway Interpretive Centre. It opens its doors to the River Art Gallery, to the Canal Café, and to volunteers who welcome seasonal visitors. Today, the Tindale-Lockmaster's house looks out toward the Seaway Iroquois lock, a symbol of our proud history.

In the Iroquois United Church Cemetery, established in 1797, situated west of the Lockmaster's house, is a plaque erected a number of years ago to recognize our heritage, to honour our ancestors and to inspire us to follow them. It reads:

"Dedicated to the Loyalists and Pioneers who settled in Dundas County. They labored and loved so that we have something to inherit and build upon".

The Cross Home and the Marina

One of the Ontario Hydro rehabilitation program features was to ensure the future safety of the new communities. It was expected that when the water would rise it would reach a level of two hundred forty-two feet (73.8 m) above sea level. An additional eight feet (2.4 m) of land elevation was reserved by Ontario Hydro as a buffer zone between the new river edge and the new communities about to be created. The new Highway #2 would be the dividing line to two hundred fifty feet (76.2 m) above sea level.

Consequently, no home or business would be built on the land south of the Highway #2. This area, considered Crown Land, would be transformed into parkland designed to support the local flora and fauna and to be used by area residents, visitors, and tourists.

The only allowed development along the new Highway #2 east of Long Sault and south of Highway #2, was the Cross home and marina, as well as the future small development on Robin Road, across the bay.

There was a home, a marina, and two cottages on the property south of Aultsville, on the St. Lawrence River, belonging to Robin and Luella Cross. As it had to be expropriated, through an agreement with Ontario Hydro the property was exchanged, although for only half its size. The old home, the marina, and the cottages were sold.

The new property, now situated south of County Road #2, faces the village of Long Sault. Considering that the marina was the only business which was operating on the water prior to the Seaway project, the Cross's were allowed to build a home and a marina on their new property.

During the construction "in the dry" of the new marina, more than a half mile (.8 km) from the old riverside, the waterfront was completely out of sight. Moreover, land had to be removed from what was to be the bay to ensure adequate water depth for the new marina. After the relocation, the depth of the bay proved inadequate for the development of a marina in the new community. Dredging of the bay caused additional expenses.

Mr. Cross applied for and was given permission to subdivide the property on the opposite side of the bay as a means to recuperate expenses associated with the relocation. These lots were later sold by Mr. Cross and the new owners applied to have the road named "Robin Road".

Mr. Cross had a fleet of tour boats which he operated, from the marina, until the late 1960's. Residents and visitors were given the opportunity to have a closer look at the seaway, the control dam, and the Moses-Saunders power generating station. During the trip, they were told about the 1958 flooding, the Seaway and Power project, as well as the history of the Lost Villages.

Thus, were created the Robin Road development and the marina project.

Parklands, our Forest Home

One aspect of the rehabilitation program was the creation, in 1955, of the St. Lawrence Parks Commission, an agency of the Province of Ontario, and the development of parklands along the new shores of the St. Lawrence River. Nine major parks including more than forty-two miles (67.2 km) of pathways along the St. Lawrence River from east of Lancaster to Iroquois were created - Glengarry Island, Ault Island, Mille Roches Island, Woodlands Island, Farran Park, Morrison Island, Crysler Memorial Park, Morrisburg Park, and Iroquois Park. These several thousand acres reserved for recreation were fully graded with sandy beaches spreading into the waters of the St. Lawrence River. Furthermore, with their fabulous scenery, numerous picnic and camping areas, these waterfront parks cross through the Lost Villages Museum and through the Upper Canada Village Museum.

Raising the water level, in 1958, to an elevation of two hundred forty-two feet (73.8 m) above sea level resulted in the redesigning of the shore lines and in the creation of twenty new islands. These three thousand five hundred acres of land, vested in the Crown, were preserved as a green belt. In 1956, the Department of Lands and Forests, as a first step of a twenty-five year plan, planted 100,000 seedlings.

In 1954 and 1955, two botanists from the Canadian Department of Agriculture studied plant life in the Seaway Valley. They concluded that this area had been one of the last regions to receive plant life in the prehistoric glacial plain, that there was no unique plant life in this region, and that there was the distinct possibility that certain plant life would disappear from the region after the flood.

Therefore, the rehabilitation program included a sustainable environment for the local fauna and flora. The migratory bird sanctuary, situated between Morrisburg and Ingleside, was created. Its objective was to preserve the local fauna and flora, and to educate by organizing year-round events which would also be entirely animated by volunteers. Built on Jack Alguire's land, purchased by Ontario Hydro, the wild fowl sanctuary and its bird migratory park, the Nairn, and Morrison islands, extending further into the St. Lawrence River, were designed to provide semi-private camping and nature environments for various groups.

Moreover, Camp Kagama, founded in 1936 on Sheek's Island by Narcisse McLaren who had spent a part of his life as a Bible Society spokesperson, became a place for holidaying, swimming, fishing, and a children's summer camp. Founded by Reverend Narcisse McLaren, Pastor, Camp Kagama opened its doors to younger and older groups of citizens in search of a summer holiday and retreat. Reverend McLaren passed away on April 5, 1945.

Camp Kagama was moved and resettled on Morrison Island during the Seaway and Power project. It continued to be managed and sponsored by a number of churches and their volunteers. A building, named McLaren Hall, was erected, soon to be followed by a number of other facilities. The first camp was held in 1961. Considering that the camp is situated on Crown Land, thus cannot be privately owned, it is now supported by a volunteer board of Directors and is open all summer to various groups.

A network of nine man-made islands joining the two new towns of Long Sault and Ingleside, on a seven mile (11.2 km) stretch of scenic parkway, were created. They were connected by a number of causeways to create the famous Long Sault Parkway with its eastern entrance at Long Sault and its western entrance at Ingleside. Their names are reminiscent of our history and heritage - Woodlands, Long Sault, Fraser, Hoople, Heriot, Vankoughnet, Phillpotts, MacDonell, Moulinette, and Mille Roches.

Residents and visitors enjoy summer camping, boating, fishing, and snorkling in the waters of the river near the new parklands.

All the parks, the islands of the Long Sault Parkway, and the other islands were named in honour of the historic Lost Villages, and those families who create new villages and build new communities.

The Ancestral Home Museum - Upper Canada Village

East of Morrisburg, west of Ingleside, north of the grounds of the historic Crysler Battlefield Memorial Park is the Upper Canada Village Museum complex. It is composed of the Upper Canada Village Museum, the Pioneer Memorial Cemetery, The Crysler Farm Battle Grounds, the Loyalist Memorial, and the Queen Elizabeth Rose Garden.

The museum was created to portray life in the early settlements along the St. Lawrence River and to preserve the atmosphere of a mid-nineteenth century community. It was developed as a living memorial to our United Empire Loyalist ancestors who settled this part of Eastern Ontario at the end of the 18th century.

Its construction began in the late 1950s and it opened its doors to the public in June, 1961. The Museum houses historically restored homes, some barns, two churches, a school house, and trade shops. With its engine house, its sawmill, its bakery, its blacksmith shop, its cabinet maker shop, its Union cheese factory, flour and woollen mills, it has brought our past history to life. Interpreters and craftspeople demonstrate, explain, and show the ways in which the people of the 1860s lived in their typical river front communities. Although most buildings came from the flooded areas of Eastern Ontario, the Museum houses a number of carefully crafted reproduction buildings brought in from other areas of Eastern Ontario, to add to its historical representation.

Based on a proposal written, in 1943, by Norman Wilson, an engineer from Toronto, the Honorable George Challis, Chairman of the Parks Development Commission, suggested in the 1950s that a historic village should be a prominent feature of our parks system. James B. Smart, who had been director of National Parks, became the Vice-Chairman of the Commission and consultant on the project. Together with Professor Anthony Adamson of the University of Toronto's school of architecture, who chose the site for the new Upper Canada Village complex, Jeanne Minhinnick and Peter J. Stokes, as well as other professionals, pursued the realization of the project throughout the late 1950s.

In an attempt to faithfully depict life of early Canada, historians, architects, furniture specialists, horticulturalists, and various other professionals were hired. Archival documents, family journals and records, diaries, and professional journals have been researched. Every effort has been made to represent an authentic picture of the 1860s. In addition, Upper Canada Village is the depository of a large archival record of some of the founding families, not only of this area, but of Ontario itself. Indeed, the Museum is the repository of our rich cultural and pioneer heritage.

Situated at the entrance of the museum is the A.L. Feader storefront moved from Wales. Today the building houses a giftshop and a snack bar, but in its heyday, the Feader store, like many mid-century general stores, was attached to the owner's home and expanded as the business grew. Built in 1820, the family home was expanded in 1840 with a porch added to it and again, in 1860, the owner erected an imposing brick structure with a storage warehouse. In the storefront window and door with its original door latch, we can still see the owner's name.

The Pioneer Memorial Cemetery is an area surrounded by walls into which tombstones of early pioneer families are encased in brick and mortar from destroyed homes and buildings. At the entrance of the grounds of the Upper Canada Village Museum, and also maintained by the Parks Commission, is a Rose Garden featuring hundreds of varieties of roses, magnolias, and other flowers which was given, as a present, to Queen Elizabeth II on her visit to the province for the Bicentennial year, in 1984. The park fountain is from Montreal Expo 67.

The Museum attracts more than three hundred thousand visitors each season during its peak years. It also offers educational programs to hundreds of school children each year and has recently introduced "Alight at Night" winter holiday season event which allows thousands more to see the Village alight with holiday festive lights from early December to early January.

The Home of the Lost Villages Museum

The Lost Villages Museum, home of the Lost Villages Historical Society, was created in 1982 by former residents of the Lost Villages. The Society was envisioned at a meeting, held in 1977, in the home of Wilda and Donald Stuart, a descendant of Doctor James Stuart, a United Empire Loyalist.

Inspired by one of its former late presidents, Françoise Laflamme, teacher and historian, some former residents of the Lost Villages shared a strong desire to create a Society which would preserve, collect, and promote our rich Eastern Ontario heritage. Following the setting of a few objectives, the Museum was, thereafter established in Ault Park, west of Cornwall. The park was named after the original Ault Park situated on Sheek's Island and flooded during the Seaway and Power project.

Donated by the McLeod family to the community, and thanks to the generosity of Lionel Grant, Cornwall Gravel, and Donald McLeod, the museum opened its doors, in 1982, with the first relocated building, the McLeod family log home originally situated near Cornwall.

The museum is also the home of the Moulinette Train Station, the Zina Hill Barber Shop from Moulinette, the Manson/Lapierre General Store from Mille Roches, the Ernie MacDonald blacksmith shop, a Corn Crib, the SS # 17 Roxborough Schoolhouse, St-David's Church driveshed from Wales, the Advent Church from Sandtown, and the newly acquired Forbes Memorial Reading Room building from Newington.

The Fran Laflamme Memorial Resource Room, in the Forbes Memorial Reading Room, is the location for the Society's archives. Indeed, on October 19, 1998, Miss Françoise Laflamme was recognized by the Ontario Heritage Foundation for her tireless enthusiasm for preserving, protecting, and promoting Eastern Ontario's heritage. She was awarded the "Heritage Community Recognition".

The basement archive room has been named the Ontario Hydro /Ontario Power Generation Room, in recognition of the generosity of these organizations.

Historical, financial, and generous volunteer donations have contributed to the successful implementation of a Museum dedicated to our ancestors. Moreover, numerous families and individuals continually support the Society and its goals.

Local visitors and tourists from all over the world arrive by bus tours, by car, and bycicle to the Museum to visit or to participate in its numerous events. The Museum is the site of numerous activities throughout the year. Guides, local walking tours, as well as bus tours, are organized through the Museum and the region of the Lost Villages.

Cultural events such as the Apples and Art Tour, the celebration of traditional Christmas music, and summer family reunions are held on site. The Sandtown Advent Church hosts a number of private weddings yearly. Along with the tours, the archival materials available help tourists and visitors to appreciate and to learn about the rich local history which the museum proudly displays. Indeed, the Society continually provides precious genealogical information to families in search of their roots.

In addition, through its monthly historically rich newsletters and meetings, Society members stay in touch and keep alive the memories of neighbours and friends.

The Lost Villages Historical Society continues to be the driving force behind the preservation, and promotion of our rich heritage with a number of activities designed to improve the Museum facilities and expand its reach.

Glossary of Architectural Terms

Bay - an opening in the façade of a dwelling.

Belvedere or cupola - a domed turret used as a lookout in a rooftop.

Bracket - a horizontal projection support often used decoratively under an eave.

Cresting - decorative vertical projection often made of iron used on porches, decks, or roof ridges and towers in Victorian homes.

Dormer - window projecting from the roof to enhance lighting of an upper storey home.

Eave - horizontal termination of a sloping roof.

Fanlight - a round or semi-elliptical transom window usually above a doorway in a radiating shape.

Flemish brickwork - a pattern created by alternating layers of bricks horizontally lengthwise (stretchers) or sideways (headers).

Gable - the underside of the triangular end of a sloping roof.

Gambrel - a ridged roof with two pitches.

Georgian - an architectural style featuring a one or two-storeys, rectangular house with a symmetrical façade of three, five or seven bays evenly spaced on either side of a front door with side lights and a transom. There were chimneys on either end of a gambrel roof line with some gables. It was designated after the four British kings named George who reigned successively during the eighteenth century.

Gothic - a style of architecture popular from the twelfth to the fifteenth centuries featuring pointed arches.

Hip roof - style of roof sloping on all four sides, also referred to as cottage roof.

Loyalist - a style of architecture developed in Upper Canada featuring a cumulative style of Western European architecture developed under the reigns of the first three British kings named George. Some characteristics are a center hall plan, one or two-storeys in height, and a balanced façade featuring a central entrance doorway with side lights and a fan transom above. The loyalist front door open from the inside only. Building materials were either wood, stone or bricks.

Neo-classic - an architectural style featuring a well proportioned rectangular building with a low-pitched gable roof or a square hip-roof building, and a balanced façade. The style popularized by the Scottish architect, Robert Adam, during the mid-eighteenth century, featured semi-elliptical transoms and side lights highlighting a front door.

Palladian - a decorative window style developed by a group of post-Renaissance architects and designers known as the Palladians, especially Andrea Palladio (1508-1580), who reinterpreted elements of the classical and roman periods into architecture. It features an arch above the center window with two additional narrow rectangular windows on either side.

Palatinate - a German territory situated along the Rhine River from which a large number of immigrants arrived in London in 1709, then to North America to settle in the north-eastern region. The term "Palatine" is used indiscriminately to the other immigrants from Germany, although they may be originating from neighboring territories.

Quoins - decorated cornerstones at the junction of two walls often made of a different material from that of the wall.

Regency - a building style popularized in the early 1830s featuring a one or one-and-a-half storey dwelling, first-floor tall windows, wide chimneys, low-hip or gable roofs, and verandas. The term regency refers to the Regency period when George IV was the British regent.

Revival - a number of building styles which evolved from the mid-eighteenth century to the 1900s, rooted in the growing interest in the arts of the early Greece and Rome featuring the Classic, the Gothic, the Italianate, the Victorian, and the Queen Anne. These periods produced more elaborate dwellings featuring irregular floor plans, various decorative elements, various roof styles, including towers and belvederes, iron cresting, front gables, wrap-around verandas, sometimes an open portico or porch with columns across the façade resulting in a temple effect. Simpler designs evolved across Canada until the first World War when homes were one or one-and-a-half storeys high with a gable facing the street and an off center front door off a ground-floor porch.

Riprap - a manner of building a stone wall or foundation where stones are thrown together irregularly.

Saltbox - a home style featuring a two-storey dwelling in the front and a one-storey high at the rear, with identical roof pitches in both directions and the ridge well toward the front.

Sidelight - a vertical window flanking a front door.

Transom - a rectangular feature above a door or window.

Trellis or treillage - a screenwork design made of wood often decorating veranda posts or supporting a porch roof.

Umbrage - an outdoor recessed area created by projections in the front and sides of a dwelling.

Wing or tail - a building extension used as a summer kitchen, wood-shed or carriage-house.

Bibliography

Archives - Upper Canada Village Museum, Lost Villages Museum, Cornwall Library Reference Center, Cornwall Standard-Freeholder Newspaper, The Morrisburg Leader Newspaper

Belden, H. & Co. Illustrated Historical Atlas of the Counties of Stormont, Dundas and Glengarry, Ontario, Illustrated, 1879. Mika Silk Screening Limited, Bellevile, Ontario, 1972

Bowering, Ian. Cornwall: From Factory Town to Seaway City. Standard-Freeholder, Cornwall, Ontario, 1999.

Bowering, Ian. Bowering's Guide to Eastern Ontario: A Cultural and Historical Companion. Quarry Press, Kingston, Ontario, 1992.

Boyle, Terry. Under This Roof, Doubleday, Toronto, Canada, 1980.

Brown, Andrew H. National Geographic magazine, Washington, U.S.A. Vol. CXV, No. 3, March 1959. Pages 299-339.

Champeau, Nicole V. Mémoire des Villages Engloutis: la Voie Maritime du Saint-Laurent de Mille Roches aux Mille-Iles. Vermillion, Ottawa, Ontario, 1999.

Chevrier, Lionel. The St. Lawrence Seaway. The MacMillan Company of Canada Limited, Toronto, 1959.

Croil, James. Dundas or a Sketch of Canadian History, and more Particularly of the County of Dundas, one of the Earliest Settled Counties in Upper Canada. B. Dawson & Son, Montreal, 1861.

Dawes, C.H. Just Being Around: Reminiscences of a Small Town United Church Minister, West Wind Press. Edmonton, Alberta, 1988.

Detzer, Karl. North America Digs a Big Ditch. The Reader's Digest, November, 1956.

Doheny-Farina, Stephen. The Grid and the Village. Yale University Press, New Haven and London, 2001.

Goldring, Philip (Staff Historian), Historic Sites and Monuments Board of Canada: Agenda Paper "Lost Villages of the St. Lawrence". St. Lawrence Parks Commission, 1986.

Guillet, Edwin C. Pioneer Days in Upper Canada, Canadian University Paperbooks Edition, 1964.

Guillet, Edwin C. Pioneer Settlements. Ontario Publishing company, 1947.

Harkness, John Graham. Stormont, Dundas and Glengarry, A History. Mutual Press Limited. Ottawa, Ontario, 1946.

Hoople, Elizabeth & the Wood Research Team. Jonas Wood, UEL. Stormont, Dundas & Glengarry Historical Society, Cornwall, Ontario, 1984.

Humphreys, Barbara, A. & Sykes, Meredith. The Buildings of Canada: A Guide to Pre-20th-Century Styles in Houses, Churches and Other Structures. The Reader's Digest Association, Montreal, 1974, 1980.

Ingram Judson, Clara. St. Lawrence Seaway, Follet Publishing Company, New York, 1959.

Introduction by Rubicam, Milton, The Old United Empire Loyalists List. Genealogical Publishing Co., Baltimore, 1969. (First published by Rose Publishing Co. Toronto, 1885 as "Centennial of the Settlement of Upper Canada by the UEL 1784-1884.)

Jeacle, Jean. To Make a House a Home. Jean Jeacle, 1975.

Jenkins, Phil. River Song: Sailing the History of the St. Lawrence. Penguin Books Canada Limited, Toronto, Canada, 2001.

Kalman, Harold. A Concise History of Canadian Architecture. Oxford University Press, 2000.

Lapp, Eula C. United Empire Loyalists Camden Valley, New York to Upper Canada. Global Heritage Press, 2000.

Livingston, Mildred Ruth. Upper Canada, Sons and Daughters of United Empire Loyalists, Vol. 1. Brown & Martin Ltd. Kingston, Ontario, 1981.

Lovell, John. The Canada Directory for 1857 - 58: Containing Names of Professional and Business Men, and of the Principal Inhabitants, in the Cities, Towns and Villages Throughout the Province; Alphabetical Directories. Printed and Published by John Lovell, St. Nicholas Street, Montreal, 1857.

Macdonald, Duncan (Darby), <u>Petitions, Land Grants and Land Petitions for the Counties of Glengarry, Stormont, and Dundas.</u> Cancopy, Toronto, Ontario, 1996.

MacRea, Marion & Adamson, Anthony. <u>The Ancestral Roof: Domestic Architecture of Upper Canada.</u> Clarke, Irwin & Company Limited, Toronto, Vancouver, 1963.

Marin, Clive & Marin, Frances. <u>Stormont, Dundas and Glengarry, 1945 - 1978.</u> Mika Publishing Company, Belleville, Ontario, 1982.

McCleod, D. <u>A Brief Review of the Settlement of Upper Canada,</u> Mika Silk Printing Limited, Belleville, Ontario, 1972.

O'Dette, Leonard A. <u>Glimpses, Glances, Sideswipes of Dickinson's Landing.</u> T & H Printers, Ottawa, 1982.

Pringle, Jacob F. <u>Lunenburg or the Old Eastern District.</u> Mika Silk Screening Limited, Belleville, Ontario, 1972.

Reid, William D. <u>The Loyalists in Ontario: The Sons and Daughters of the American Loyalists of Upper Canada.</u> Hunterdon House, Lambertville, New Jersey, 1973.

Reid, Thomas H. & Boulton William, D. <u>St. Lawrence Seaway and Power Projects 1959.</u> Reid and Boulton Publishing Co. Montreal, Canada, 1958.

Ripley, Donald M. <u>Gateway to the World; A Picture Story of the St. Lawrence Seaway.</u> Chomedy Publications Ltd., Montreal, Canada, 1959.

Senior, Elinor K. <u>From Royal Township to Industrial City.</u> Mika Publishing Company, Belleville, Ontario, 1983.

Smith, H.M. Scott. <u>The Historic Houses of Prince Edward Island.</u> SS Publications, Halifax, Nova Scotia, 1990.

Smyth Carter, J. <u>The Story of Dundas: Being a History of the County of Dundas from 1784 to 1904.</u> The St. Lawrence News Publishing House, 1905.

Stephens, George W. <u>The St. Lawrence Waterway Project: The Story of the St. Lawrence River as an International Highway for Water-borne Commerce.</u> Louis Carrier & Co. Ltd., Montreal/London/New York, 1930.

Stiles, H.M. <u>Official History of the Cornwall Cheese and Butter Board.</u> Cornwall Cheese and Butter Board, 1919.

Rutley, Rosemary. <u>Voices from the Lost Villages.</u> Casa Maria Publications, Maxville, Ontario, 1998.

St. Andrew's Historical Society Bicentennial Committee. <u>Heritage Highlights of Cornwall Township.</u> Minuteman Press, Cornwall, 1984.

United Empire Loyalists Association of Canada. <u>Loyal She Remains: A Pictorial History of Canada.</u> Toronto, Ontario, 1984.

Webber, Annie E. <u>Newington, Osnabruck, Stormont County, 1826 - 1987.</u> Webber, Annie E., 1989.

Wickware Morgan, Eleanor. <u>Up the Front: a Story of Morrisburg.</u> Ryerson Press, Toronto, 1964.

White, Arthur V. <u>Commission of Conservation Canada, Committee on Waters and Water-Powers, Long Sault Rapids: St. Lawrence River: An Inquiry into the Constitutional and Other Aspects of the Project to Develop Power Therefrom.</u> Printed by the Mortimer Co. Limited, Ottawa, 1913.